The Central Zone

Also by Fred Glasbrenner,
Journey of a Lifetime.

The Central Zone

*a memoir
about abalone diving
by one of the first to start
this incredible industry in
Victoria*

Friedrich Glasbrenner

ISBN: 978-0-6488801-5-8

First edition ©2022, Friedrich (Fred) Glasbrenner.

Published by F & Z Glasbrenner
603/50 Saltwater Promenade
Point Cook
Victoria 3030.

Book design, preparation, and editing by John Litchen
3 Firestone Court, Robina, Qld 4226.
All photos are from the collections of F Glasbrenner, Ken Johnson, and John Litchen.

Dedication:

This one is for my great diving mate Ken Johnson (Rommy Statkus) who sadly is no longer with us. We were diving partners for more than eight years and friends forever. We shared some great adventures in New Guinea, out in the ocean during a cyclone at Middleton Reef, and in the Arabian Gulf, among others.

True friends are rare in this world, and Kenny was a true friend. He will be missed by all who knew him.

Table of contents

- 7 - Foreword Port Phillip Bay and its great potential
- **9 - Part One - Early Days**
- 11 - From Bus driver to diver
- 15 - Our first professional dive
- 18 - Our first serious attempt at becoming abalone divers
- 29 - Surprises
- 31 - Branching out
- 34 - Nothing short of disaster
- 37 - One more surprise
- 39 - An idea forms
- 41 - A pat on the back
- 43 - A minor setback
- 47 - A mess under the pier
- **63 - Part Two - Port Phillip Bay**
- 64 - We made a great team
- 71 - A totally different ball game
- 72 - New Suits
- 73 - Unexpected changes
- **77 - Part Three - More adventures in The Bay and in Bass Straight**
- 78 - Getting back into it
- 79 - A fish story
- 83 - A new boat
- 85 - Back on the Mintak
- 92 - Going separate ways - A new beginning
- 96 - A serious threat appears
- 104 - More regulations
- **105 - Part Four - A New Venture**
- 106 - The birth of AAE: Australian Abalone Exports
- 110 - Plans approved
- 111 - Victorian Abalone Divers Association
- 111 - Another threat
- 113 - A new boat and a mooring
- 120 - The Francis
- 125 - Transferability ... at Last!
- 126 - Exciting times
- 128 - Diving at Cape Schanck
- 144 - Feeling Happy
- 145 - and Excited
- 155 - A new Era Begins
- 159 - Opening Day
- 162 - Something different
- 168 - A fish and chip shop
- 172 - Doing what we were meant to do
- 182 - No longer alone
- 186 - A worldwide shortage
- 188 - Building the world's largest abalone
- 196 - The man-made artificial reef of Altona
- 204 - Brad Adams - Ocean Abalone Rancher
- 206 - But life goes on...
- 209 - A surprise package
- 212 - New customers
- 215 - Selling AAE, the final chapter
- 218 - Acknowledgments

Foreword

Port Phillip Bay and it's great Potential

With 1,930 square kilometres of pristine waters serviced by the Great Southern Ocean, Port Phillip Bay is the biggest inland bay in the world. Where else can one jump in a 'tinny' and a few meters from shore catch a big snapper, a gummy shark, some nice flatties, or a fighting yellow tail kingfish at any tick of the clock?

Although used extensively by thousands of fishermen both professional as well as amateur, by *boaties* of every persuasion, *yachties*, swimmers, skin divers, scuba divers and snorkelers, people who love to walk along a beach and find shells, run with their dogs, and anyone who just goes to the seaside to look at the vast expanse of water in the bay, it still has enormous unrealized potential. People living in and around the Port Phillip Bay are in my view, the luckiest people on our planet.

My Name is Friedrich (Fred) Glasbrenner and my hope is that someone reading this memoir about abalone diving will feel the same thrills that I have had experiencing the wonder that is above and under our Port Phillip Bay.

I think of myself as being fortunate to be among the first explorers who ventured underwater in Port Phillip Bay.

In hindsight I now realize how, at that time, I was able to appreciate what The Bay had to offer, and knew then that if we didn't manage it correctly, we could lose it. Those sentiments are even more important today.

Part One
Early days

Friedrich Glasbrenner

Somewhere under the surface in Port Phillip Bay.

A small stingray patrols its territory inside Port Phillip Bay Heads.

From bus driver to diver

I started in 1958 as a skindiver using just a mask, a snorkel, and swim-fins (flippers) which I attribute to being invented by Hans Hass, an Austrian marine biologist and pioneer in underwater exploration and photography. I was at that time a bus driver on the Mooney Ponds Williamstown line, and when parked at Williamstown I saw two guys coming out of the water at the Crystal Pool. They were dripping wet, had their masks pushed up on top of their heads with the snorkels dangling behind, and holding fins in their hands. The two guys were John Litchen and his Canadian friend George Olah.

"It's bloody freezing," I heard one of them say.

There was a cold southerly blowing and so coming out of cold sea water must have been really cold.

I introduced myself and we started talking. It was both of them who convinced me to give skindiving a go. John was a member of the Bulldogs Skindiving Club and he later became my brother-in-law. George, who was a phenomenal snorkeler became the best man at my wedding to John's sister Zara.

I didn't need that much convincing to go into the water. I had already done some diving years before in the Mediterranean on a trip with two friends in a boat crossing the sea from Sicily to Tunisia in North Africa.

But diving in Port Phillip Bay was something different entirely. To begin with, the water was so much colder and you needed some kind of protection to keep warm. It would be a few years before wet-suits were invented, but what was available were wraparound rubber things called *seal-skins*, under which you had to wear jumpers to keep warm, and dry suits, frogman suits, manufactured by Pirelli in Italy. If you accidentally punctured them by bumping into or being scraped against sharp rocks underwater, they rapidly filled with icy water and caused major problems. If you went too deep, the water compressing the suit against you pinched your skin, and we sometimes had terrible marks on our legs as a result.

George Olah, wearing his Pirelli dry suit grabbing a spear gun in preparation to going into the water

John Litchen, wearing thermal air-cell underwear, socks, and a thick jumper before putting on his Pirelli dry suit.

Fred, just out of the water at Barwon Heads, holding a speared fish in one hand and a crayfish in the other.

Even before we had any kind of suit, we jumped into the water wearing only bathers, and equipped with a rubber powered spear-gun, we never came home without a couple of nice fish for dinner. On weekends we dived off the rocks at Queenscliff, or in the ocean if it was flat. We loved Barwon Heads, just off the bluff where crayfish abounded. We often went as far as Cape Schanck where George was a master at free-diving amongst the bommies to search for big Southern Crays, or lobsters as the Americans called them. Australian crayfish (from the ocean) don't have claws as do the American ones.

On nice summer weekends we would spend the time at Mount Martha, sleeping on the beach, diving and hand collecting scallops, or shooting some fish, all of which we would cook on an open fire with a grill right there on the beach. It was a fabulous time. There was plenty of seafood for everyone no matter where you went in the water.

Fred, John, and a friend's children eating scallops cooked on the beach at Mt Martha.

I became a fanatical skindiver and spent every spare moment underwater. As a bus driver on the Mooney Ponds, Footscray, Williamstown Beach run, I was in the water in the mornings before my afternoon shift, or immediately after finishing if I was doing the early shift.

You couldn't help noticing whenever you were in the water that every reef was covered with abalone, mussels, baby clams or other shellfish. Often abalone sat on top of other abalone and Port Jackson sharks and banjo sharks would work their way along the reef trying to prise off the shellfish in order to eat them. One day I saw net fishermen throwing back into the water some abalone that had been tangled in their nets.

"Why throw it back?" I asked one of them.

The look he gave me told me he thought I must have been simple-minded to ask such a question. "Because it's mutton fish," he said abruptly, as if that was all the explanation needed. When he saw me looking puzzled, he added, "they're no good for anything, not even bait."

These guys simply had no idea of the potential that was there in the bay, if it wasn't a 'proper' fish, then it was rubbish and was thrown back into the water.

Not everyone thought like those fishermen. Frank Mathews, who had a small canning factory in Mordialloc in the late 1950s was diving with a young Clark Espie for bay mussels and scallops, and he canned them for the local market. Frank's friend, Peter Thompson, the Australian Golf Champion, asked him if he ever came across **awabi**, which is what the Japanese call abalone

"The ocean and the Bay out there are full of them, Frank said, "but no one wants them. Apparently, a few people had tried to cook them but couldn't eat them because they were as tough as nails."

"Maybe you should try canning them," Peter suggested.

Frank and Clarke went out dived in the ocean off Sorrento and collected some abalone and made a few cans as an experiment; which as far as I know, makes them the first abalone divers in Australia. Peter took some of the cans to Japan when he went on another golf tournament. He gave them to restaurant owners to try and was surprised at the positive outcome. But at that time there was plenty of fresh *awabi* in Japan and no one considered the cooked and canned product. Nothing came of it, and Frank continued with his canned mussels.

Frank Mathews years later at his home in Tasmania reminiscing with a glass of red wine.

Frank Mathews' can of Abalone Soup. This was on display at a special Abalone Industry seminar in Hobart Tasmania in 2005. The can was obviously showing its age, and no one would consider opening it. It was the only one of its kind left.

It took a couple of years before a few canning companies like Safcol, Ocean Garden, Russel Crayfish, SPC, and Smorgons started to show an interest in canning abalone. Since Smorgons were located in Somerville Road, not far from us, I visited them to inquire if they would be interested in buying fresh abalone. They said they were, and would pay two shillings a pound on weekdays.

My fitness levels were good. I could easily dive to twenty metres holding my breath and stay down there for a minute, so I figured I would have no trouble collecting a few bucket loads of abalone. I mentioned how much Smorgons would pay to my two diving buddies, Wally and Peter, and we decided we would have a go on the next good diving day. We bought big screw drivers from a local hardware store, drilled holes in the handles so we could tie a cord to attach the screw driver to our wrists. We got spatulas for shucking the abs, and plastic buckets to put them in. We were ready to become professional abalone divers; at least that's what we thought. We were excited and couldn't wait to get started.

Our first professional dive

It was September 1963, three months before I was to get married, early in the morning when we first dived for abalone on a small reef inside of the Gellibrand Lighthouse, off the back of Williamstown. We wore dry suits to keep us warm, and we only used masks, snorkels, and fins.

It was a hell of a day. The water was freezing and after a couple of hours none of us could feel our fingers. We each had a potato sack which we swam out to the reef with, and as we dived and collected the abalone it went into the potato sack, and when that was full, we had to swim back to shore, grab another sack and repeat the process. It was harder than we imagined.

By the time we'd filled a couple of sacks each we had a few onlookers who'd been walking along the back beach who wanted to know what we were going to do with all the mutton fish.

"We're selling them to a cannery."

"Really?" One of the onlookers said. "Who would eat that stuff?"

"You'd be surprised," was all I could think of saying.

Extracting the abalone from the shell, shucking, for the first time was difficult.

The people watching us soon got bored and wandered off along the beach.

We sat on some rocks by the water's edge and as we shucked each abalone, the shell and the guts were thrown into the water which instantly attracted schools of tiny fish that swarmed all over the stuff. It took us a while to get the hang of it, so we didn't waste as much of the good part, the meat of the abalone as we had at the beginning.

We ended up with 4 large buckets of shucked abalone, and using Peter's panel van, we delivered it to Smorgons just in time to catch them before closing. They weighed it, and we had 290 pounds. They handed us a chit with the weight recorded and told us to come back and pick up our money in a couple of days.

It said nothing about how much we would be paid, only recorded the weight.

Two days later I turned up at the office to be met by a guy called Harry Humphreys.

"Where did you get those abs from?" he asked.

"From Port Phillip Bay by the old lighthouse. The reefs there are full of them. Why?"

"They're no good," he said. "Too dark; what we consider to be third grade."

"Third grade?" I had no idea what that meant.

"We can only pay you 7 pennies a pound."

That was a bit of a downer. Less than a third of what we were expecting.

"Don't bring us any more like that. What we want is abalone from the ocean."

He paid me eight pounds and two shillings in cash, and that meant that we each got just a bit more than two and a half quid (Pounds). And for that we had to work really hard. If I did an extra shift on my day off from driving the bus, I would earn five pounds, and if it was on a Sunday, seven pounds, and that's easy, just sitting in a bus and driving. It was certainly a letdown, to think we could make a fortune from our hobby, but in hindsight it was worth a try. I think we were the first divers to sell abalone from the Bay.

In January 1964 Zara and I got married, and we put a deposit down (with substantial help from Zara's parents) on a brick veneer house in North Altona. The area had yet to be sewered and the roads were not finished. It took us fifteen years to pay it off.

It may not have looked too impressive at first, but it was ours. It didn't take long before the streets were surfaced and that made a big difference.

Every spare moment I had saw me snorkeling in the Bay. Zara, who at that time was a **Tivoli** dancer and later a **Lido** Showgirl, often joined me on her days off.

Friedrich Glasbrenner

Our first serious attempt at becoming abalone divers

1964/65/66 were the years when skindiving and spearfishing started to become very popular, and dive shops were established all over Australia. A couple of companies started to manufacture three-piece foam rubber wetsuits. The pants, the jacket and the hood were glued rather than sown, but they looked good. I didn't waste any time in getting the three pieces and it finally felt great to be warm and comfortable in the water, (without the suit pinching the skin as dry suites under pressure did). Of course, it had to be weighted, like the dry suits, but the wet suit was much easier to put on and take off than the earlier dry suits had been, so I was happy about that.

It was about the middle of August 1965 when someone told me that an Englishman with an eighteen-foot dive boat wanted a couple of divers to collect abalone. I got his address, which was not far from where we lived, so Peter and I visited him in West Footscray. His name was Fred, and he was middle aged. He had heard that Safcol in Footscray bought abalone from a guy called Les Stephan in Cape Everard, near the Cann River, just south of Mallacoota. Fred was happy to meet us and to show us his boat, which he had fitted out himself as a dive boat. Driven by a75 horsepower Evinrude outboard motor, winched onto a galvanized single axle trailer, pulled by a four-wheel drive Land Rover Wagon, it looked very impressive.

Thinking back now, I realize how primitive the setup was with a small air compressor mounted on a wooden plank across the transom, with a petrol motor to one side to drive it, with a homemade steel reserve tank on the other side. The reserve tank had a blow-off valve, a pressure gauge, a small glass water trap, a couple of hose fittings, and a small cylinder filled with rags acting as an air filter fitted to it. Two 60 feet long water hoses were curled up on the floor, and that was it.

Peter, who by this time had bought a house in Avondale Heights, was married, had two young daughters, and with his wife pregnant again, was somewhat dubious about the dive boat set up. He worked at *Containers* as a fitter and turner. Unseen to Fred, Peter pointed out to me some obvious mistakes with the diving boat setup, but kept it to himself.

I was super keen to do the diving regardless of the setup and Peter reluctantly agreed to accompany me.

Fred could not dive and was glad when he found out we had dived on bottles and were willing to join him. He reckoned he would act as a deckhand, monitoring the air supply and shelling the abs we would bring up.

It was arranged that Peter and I would take some unpaid leave from work to go abalone diving. Peter had bought a second-hand four-wheel drive International Ute, with a canopy and heaps of room for our tent, diving gear, and the rest of our luggage. We were ready to hit the road. Early the next morning we met Fred at his place and together we headed off to Cape Everard and Mallacoota to become professional abalone divers.

Wally, John and Peter, sorting out equipment to get ready to go to Cape Everard.

It worked out for me very well.

Zara was asked by the Lido management whether she would like to do a "*Conquista Rum*" and International/Harvester commercial, along with a three-week promotion for another Lido show in Sydney, with several of the showgirls. The current show only had a few days to go before rehearsals would start for a new show. Naturally Zara said yes, and she and the other girls few to Sydney the day after we left for our first abalone diving stint.

With Zara in Sydney, I could concentrate on getting ready. I couldn't believe how much we had to do but we managed and early on the third day Peter picked me up on the way to Fred's place where he was waiting for us, ready to leave as soon as we got there.

Unfortunately, the weather wasn't very kind to us. It was cold with a south-westerly blowing and every so often we got drenched with icy rain. A horrible winter's day. It was a long haul. With no automatic transmission, and no power steering, driving in windy wet weather was hard work. Every time we stopped for fuel or a bite to eat, we changed drivers, each of us taking turns. Fred said he didn't mind driving all the way, but we insisted on changing drivers to make it a bit easier for him. One thing was for sure; we would never make the 500 plus kilometres to Cape Everard by nightfall.

It was just after midday when we arrived at Lakes Entrance, a bit over half way, and that was the easy part because the highway was surfaced. Beyond Lakes Entrance, the road on to Cann River where we had to turn off to get to Cape Everard, was unpaved, rutted and corrugated even though it was supposed to be a main highway. The town itself was a timber town located on the junction of the Cann highway (from the mountains) and the Princes Highway (highway 1) about halfway between Melbourne and Sydney. There were a lot of hotels, motels and similar places because it was a place where people often stopped while on the long journey to or from Melbourne to Sydney.

When we finally arrived at Bidwell's service station in Cann River it was getting dark. We were told we would have to stay at the pub overnight because it was too dangerous to drive in the dark down to the cape through the bush on an unmade road, a track really, that was worse than what we'd already encountered. This suited us, because we were exhausted. Bidwell (I forgot his first name, but I think it was Tom) invited us for dinner and drinks at the pub and was happy to get to know us. He was the person who would be transporting our abalone to Safcol.

After breakfast, refueling and being pointed to the right track by Bidwell, we were on our way. The track was called Cape Everard track then, but was later renamed Point Hicks track. There still is and has been for years controversy over whether Captain James Cook's first sighting of Australia in 1770 was actually the cape, which he named Cape Hicks after the crewman who first saw it, but which subsequent explorers couldn't find at the position Captain Cook marked on his chart, is actually the cape he saw or a cloud bank that from a distance looked like it could be land. This is still debated by historians to this day.

The track got worse after the first couple of kilometres, and was passable only by a four-wheel drive. Fortunately, Peter's truck was a 4-wheel drive. Fred's truck was also a 4-wheel drive and he followed behind us towing his boat as we made our way along the track. I lost count of the times we had to stop to push fallen branches as big as small trees to one side so we could get past. We even had to stop sometimes to shovel rocks into a huge pothole in order to drive over it without getting bogged. It was the worst road/track I had ever driven along.

The Central Zone

The distance to the cape was around 50 kilometres, but it took hours of slow driving, stopping to clear debris, filling potholes, with lots of cursing before we finally reached our destination. We crossed a small wooden bridge and drove into a campsite. There were a couple of boats on the beach, two tents, and a nice warm campfire burning.

We were welcomed by Les Stephan and his deckhand, Charlie (Karl) Schwabeegger and Wally Kalusevisius, and his deckhand who had only arrived the day before. Les had apparently been diving earlier because we saw several plastic bins full of shucked abalone meat next to several bags of salt. He still had on his wetsuit pants, but also wore a heavy warm jumper and a knitted cap. It was very cold at the campsite with a south-westerly blowing, but the ocean was flat and great for diving.

Les pointed to a wet potato sack. "I've got a couple of big crays in there which we can cook for dinner later," he told us.

Unloading the ute to set up camp in the scrub by the beach.

We set up our camp near the fire. We unloaded our gear and then Fred backed the boat on its trailer as close as he could to the water's edge without getting bogged in the soft sand. With help from the others, we pushed the boat off the trailer and onto some wooden rollers to be ready to launch in the morning. It didn't take long to put up our tent, after which we helped Les as he weighed and salted his abs, and packed them into wet potato bags. Once that was done, we dug a couple of holes in the wet sand beside the creek under the bridge where Les buried his bags of salted abs in the cool sand to keep them fresh. After that, we boiled the crays and sat around the campfire eating this finest of fine seafood as we all got to know each other.

"You'll only get two or three days of diving before the weather changes," Les told us as we finished our crayfish. "It'll swing to the north and then come in from the east, and it all turns to shit after that. No way you'll dive once the weather turns, so make the most if it while you can."

Whatever, we couldn't wait to get started.

When we got up after a restless night, the sky was overcast, threatening to rain. Les was beside the campfire brewing coffee that smelled delicious. He still wore his wetsuit pants and the same thick jumper, which made me wonder whether he'd slept in them all night.

There was no boat ramp here and we had to push the boats in over the sand using wooden rollers underneath the bottom of the hull. It was hard work because with all the diving gear on board the boats were quite heavy. Everybody helped. There were three boats. Les was the sole diver on his along with his deckhand, Wally, Charlie and their deckhand in the second boat, with myself and Peter in Fred's boat.

In the water we followed Les along the coast a way until he stopped and threw in his anchor over a reef he'd dived on the day before.

He pointed towards a lighter patch of water and said "Try that spot over there. There's a good reef there."

We moved our boat to the spot indicated and dropped anchor.

I was extremely excited to jump into the water and could hardly wait for Fred to start the compressor. The blasted thing wouldn't start. Driven by a 2 HP Fichtel and Sachs two-stroke motor, you had to start it by pulling a cord, like a lawn mower. Fred kept pulling and pulling to no avail. Nothing happened. Peter then moved over, and turned on the petrol valve, gave the motor a couple of pulls and it started easily. He didn't say anything, but just picked up his mask and started rinsing it.

Grabbing a potato sack I slipped into the water, to discover a world unlike any I had dived in before. Very different from the Bay or the water at Barwon Heads or off Queenscliff. The visibility was phenomenal, but it was dark because there was no sun above us, just an overcast sky. The reef below was easy to see and it stretched off into the distance. It was around ten metres below and covered with long-stemmed seaweed at least half a metre high with broad leaves at the top. It swayed gently as the waves rolled over above. Swimming down through the seaweed there was beautiful abalone as far as I could see.

After admiring the scene for a few moments, I started to work. Prising off good sized abalone and putting them into the potato sack. In no time the sack was almost full and I estimated it weighed around 30 kilos. It was heavy and I had some difficulty in hauling it back up to the boat. Once at the surface, there was no way I could lift it into the boat and Fred had to lean over and pull it up as I pushed from underneath. It was a struggle, but we got it into the boat. He gave me another sack and down I went again. This time though I wouldn't put so much in before swimming it back up to the surface.

As soon as Peter and I had our first loads on board Fred started shucking the abs and throwing the shells with some gut still attached over the side. Within a few minutes there were fish everywhere. All different sizes, and colours, they attacked the falling shells and stripped every morsel that was left attached to them. It was a spectacular sight.

I think I was filling my fourth or fifth sac when the air stated to taste smoky and became difficult to breathe. A few moments later I felt my tongue get sucked into the regulator and the sudden pain stunned me. I let go of the sack I had just filled and ripped the mouthpiece off. I swam up to the surface and started coughing as soon as my head was out of the water.

Peter was climbing into the boat, and he didn't look happy. I followed him and climbed back on board.

"What the fuck happened?" I demanded to know.

"The hoses were blown," Peter said.

They had both been clamped to a T-piece which got very hot and as the rubber hoses also heated up, they produced bad poisonous air. When the hoses got too hot, they split and the sudden drop in pressure is what sucked my tongue into the mouthpiece. Peter was extremely angry and told Fred that the T-piece should have been on an extended water pipe to keep it cool. He also told Fred the air was bad because the filters were mounted incorrectly.

None of this registered on Fred who was busy cutting the blown pieces of hose and refitting them. He started the motor again and grabbed Peter's regulator, smelled the air.

"It's as good as gold," he said. "You can get back to work now. It's all fixed."

Peter definitely wasn't happy, but he grabbed his regulator and dropped back over the side. I went in after him and had no trouble finding the sack I'd dropped. There were fish all over it trying to get at the abalone. I did see a huge crayfish backing into a hole nearby with one of my abs in its claws. I swam back up with the sack and passed it to Fred. I managed to fill several more sacks before the air again started to taste foul. I had to stop then, and swam back to the boat.

When I got to the surface, I saw Peter was in the boat helping Fred shuck the abalone. Fred had been unable to keep up with both of us supplying him with sacks full of beautiful abalone. I climbed back on board and after taking off mask and flippers I started to help as well. Once we'd finished, we had 5 bins and the bailing bucket full to the brim with prime abalone. Not bad for our first day.

We packed up, and headed back to the camp. Les was already gone, and not far behind us came Wally and Charlie in their boat.

As we ran the boats up onto the sand, we saw Les arguing with someone. The man was dressed in a uniform and they were standing beside a 4-wheel drive with 'Fisheries Patrol' painted in large letters on the side. After we had unloaded our catch and pushed the boat further up onto the sand, the guy came over to us and introduced himself as Inspector (I have forgotten his name).

"I'm from the Victorian Fisheries Department, in Melbourne. Can I see your master fisherman's licence please?"

At least he was polite.

Apparently, you needed a master fisherman's licence in order to sell produce taken from the sea. We were unaware that we needed a licence. No one had mentioned anything about that to us. Even Fred had to have one, since he was working with produce from the sea, and on top of that, as the boat owner he also needed a commercial boat licence.

Come to think of it, Les had said something around the campfire the night before that we needed a licence to become professional fishermen, but we didn't take much notice of it, thinking that we would see to it once we got back to Melbourne.

"I can issue you a temporary licence right now," he said once we told him we were not aware that we needed it. "It'll cost you one pound each."

We looked at each other and wondered whether this guy was putting us on.

"It's either that, or I have to confiscate your catch."

Shit. After all the hard work we'd put in, breathing dirty air, dragging the heavy sacks back up to the boat and shucking the abs, we weren't going to let that happen. Wally and Charlie were told the same thing, but they just shrugged. They would pay the one pound.

I think if the guy hadn't been wearing an official uniform, Peter would have slugged him. He was pissed off. We still had our wetsuits on and our hands were half frozen from being in the cold water for so long. The problem was, that we didn't have any spare cash with us, which is why we were prepared to argue.

Les walked over to his tent while we were discussing the fee with the inspector. He came back with enough money to pay for us as well as Wally and Charlie.

"This should cover it," he told the inspector.

"All right," I said. "Do we get a receipt or something to prove we'd paid?"

"Of course." He pulled out a receipt book and wrote down on each receipt each person's particulars. As he handed us the receipts, he said, "When you get back to Melbourne, go to the Fisheries Department and show them the receipt. You will then be issued with a proper Master Fisherman's licence."

With that, he wished us a good day, hopped back into his vehicle and drove off back up the track towards Cann River.

"You can pay me back at the end of the run, once we get paid," Les told us.

"No worries mate, Thanks."

From that moment on, we were professional fishermen, and with all the ups and downs over subsequent years, I never regretted it for one moment.

The cost of my first Master Fisherman's licence.
One Pound, which was soon converted into two Dollars.

Finally, we could weigh our catch. Les had a set of scales mounted on the back of his truck. They were ancient looking scales, simple but effective. Still wearing our wetsuits, we hauled our bins and the bucket over to his truck and weighed everything. We had 550 pounds; a good haul.

Wally and Charlie weighed theirs and they had 100 pounds less than us. They too had experienced problems with their equipment during the dive.

Les would take our combined catches as well as his back to Bidwells at Cann River from where it would be delivered to Safcol for processing and canning.

Les gave us a receipt for 500 pounds, and when I looked at him curiously, he said, "50 pounds will be deducted for blood loss during transit."

That seemed fair enough. If we got paid for 500 pounds, it would still be a good amount, since the rate was £2-6 (2 Pounds and six shillings) per pound of Abalone.

With Les's buried abalone and our two hauls he had a total of 1500 pounds. It was still only early afternoon, so he decided he would leave immediately for Cann river to deliver the haul.

"If I go now, I can deliver it all before dark. I should be back early tomorrow morning."

We helped him load all the abs onto the back of his truck, and once he took off, we finally could get out of our wetsuits. We washed the salt off our bodies in the creek under the bridge. That water was colder than the ocean, which was unexpected, so it was a very quick wash, and into some warm clothes. As soon as we'd warmed up by the campfire Peter helped Fred make some changes to the compressor setup to prevent problems the next day. At least, that's what we hoped.

The next morning when we emerged from the tent it was very cold and misty. The sea was as flat as a shit carter's hat. (That's how Les's deckhand described it.)

After a cup of coffee and a few of Fred's sandwiches, we put on our very cold and damp wetsuits. There's nothing worse than putting on a cold wet or damp wetsuit, but we had no way of drying them since the weather itself stayed cold and damp. In summer it would be different, but it was the end of August, the end of winter, so a warm dry wetsuit to put on was not an option.

Les arrived back just as we were about to push our boat into the water.

He handed Fred £62-10 (62pounds and ten shillings) in cash for the abalone we'd got, and pointed in the general direction of the reefs where we'd dived the day before. "I'll be following you out there as soon as I can get organized."

We didn't go as far as we went the day before and as soon as we'd noticed some weed, we dropped anchor. Fred started the compressor as Peter and I grabbed our masks and put on flippers and weight belts. We were over the side and heading down a few moments later.

The first thing I saw was a huge crayfish, just waiting to be caught. I grabbed it and swam back up to the boat and gave it to Fred.

"For dinner tonight," I said.

He gave me a thumbs up, and then I went down again. The air was still pretty bad, but it was bearable. It took only a short time to fill my bag. There were abs everywhere I looked, and in hardly any time at all I had filled and ferried up to the boat several bags full, before the inevitable happened. My tongue got sucked up into the mouthpiece again. Fucking compressor, I thought as I quickly headed to the surface. When I broke the surface beside the boat, Peter was already on board arguing with Fred. They were arguing about the compressor fittings. The hose was busted again.

It took a while to repair before we could dive again.

"Look," I said to Fred, "keep an eye on the bloody hose and if it looks like busting, give us a couple of tugs on the hose before you switch off the compressor so we'll know to come up. It's no fun getting your tongue sucked up into the regulator. We could even drown."

"Sorry guys," he mumbled.

It took enough time to fill one more bag before I felt a couple of tugs on the hose. I immediately headed up with my full bag, and passed to Fred. I climbed on board; Peter was right behind me with a full bag as well. No sooner than both of us were on board the hose broke again.

"Bloody shit gear," Peter mumbled.

Fred had been unable to shuck the abs as quick as we could send up a bag full, so we sat and helped with shucking what we'd already collected. After that we decided to pack up and head back to camp. Les wasn't far behind us as we ran the boat up onto the edge of the sand.

As it turned out, we'd collected more than we had the day before, so we were quite pleased. We managed to get 760 pounds. Les gave us a receipt for 700 pounds. If it hadn't been for the bad air and the hose breaking, we could have done much better. On top of that Peter had caught two big crays to go with the one I got and as soon as we'd finished helping Les salt the meat before bagging it again (Charlie and Wally did as good as we had), we started to cook the crays.

We didn't need to bury the meat, because Les said he would deliver it the next afternoon himself, all the way to Safcol in Melbourne.

"You probably won't get much diving in tomorrow morning as an easterly change was coming, and that will stir up the water too much."

Sitting around the warm campfire, stuffing ourselves with a hot stew Les's deckhand had prepared and eating the delicious crayfish we'd caught, we thought we were living in paradise.

In the morning we got up early and didn't waste any time getting the boats into the water. But when I saw Fred's hands, I couldn't believe it. Both his thumbs and forefingers were ulcerated and swollen. He also had ulcers opening on the back of his hands.

"What happened to your hands?" I asked him. "They look terrible."

"I've no idea. I must be allergic to abalone."

"I'll be stuffed. Will you be able to drive the boat?"

"Yeah. No problem. I'll put some Band-Aids on them. Nothing keeps an Englishman down,"

By the time we got the boat out and over to a good diving spot, we noticed a swell had developed. Underwater, the visibility wasn't so good as it had been. There was a lot of stuff floating and a lot of movement of the seaweed. Peter and I worked as hard and as fast as we could.

Just as we decided to get out of the water the hose busted again, so that was the end of the day's diving. It was midday and already getting too rough to work safely. The wind had also changed. Back on board we helped Fred who was in a lot of pain shelling the abs, but we were pleasantly surprised when we weighed our catch back at the camp. We had 580 pounds, which meant Les would give us a receipt for 550 pounds weight.

When we'd finished weighing and stacking all the bags of abalone on Les's truck, the wind had become noticeably stronger. Waves were breaking onto the beach, and the ocean, as far as we could see was choppy, and getting rougher by the minute.

In the three days we'd been there, we'd each made around £60, which made me happy. It would take me three weeks driving a buss to make that same amount.

"We should break camp," Les said once his struck was fully loaded. "This easterly wind and the shitty weather will last at least a week. It'll be impossible to dive here with weather like this. You should go home. When the weather comes good again, I'll call you, okay?"

We helped Fred put his boat on the trailer and loaded up Peter's truck with the camp gear and headed back up the track to Bidwell's service station and adjacent motel.

I had convinced Peter that we should drive up to Sydney instead of going back to Melbourne. I wanted to see how Zara and the girls were getting on with their promotion for the Lido. I also wanted to catch up with George, my best man. It had been a while since I'd seen him.

After a very early breakfast we left the motel and headed up to Sydney, arriving very late in the afternoon and surprised Zara and her friends who had not been expecting me. They were staying at a small luxurious hotel in Darlinghurst, where visiting celebrities often stayed.

The girls had signed a contract with the film company and were on call at all hours to shoot the commercials. They were being paid good money so that was a bonus.

Peter and I weren't allowed to stay with them, so we had to find alternative accommodation.

Four of the Lido Girls in Sydney promoting the next show "Avec Pleasure". Zara is the third from the left.

Surprises

Peter and I drove over to George's house in Bronte where I knew we could stay, and to say he was surprised to see us was an understatement. Of course, he wasn't expecting me (and Peter) to suddenly turn up out of nowhere, but he made us very welcome. He was even more surprised when he found out we were diving for abalone just over the NSW Victorian border and wanted to hear all about it. He'd established a successful jewelery shop in Kings Cross, but whenever he had spare time, he was diving off Bronte or Tamarama. Sometimes he would collect some very big abalone and being a good amateur chef, he knew exactly how to cook them.

"I've got a big surprise for you," he said to me. "But you'll have to wait until morning."

It was already dark by this time, quite late. I couldn't help wonder what the surprise might be, but after a couple of glasses of wine and something to eat both Peter and I could hardly stay awake. We crashed on the couches in the lounge room for the night.

The surprise was the first of several that changed my life.

"Follow me," George said and he led us out onto a balcony at the back of his house.

He pointed into the back yard of his neighbor's house which the balcony overlooked.

I could hardly believe my eyes. I had to rub them several times and blinking furiously to clear them I stared at what appeared to be a whole yard covered by a fine mesh. But underneath that mesh was a number of large planks all covered with abalone drying in the fresh air. A slight breeze ruffled the netting covering the yard. I reckon there would have been a thousand abalone drying on those planks.

A Chinese man wandered out into the yard and started turning the abalone over. He looked up and saw the three of us on the balcony. "Hey George," he called out. "What's happening?"

"I've got a couple of friends I'd like you to meet."

"Bring them down," he said as he continued to turn over each abalone.

When we got down and had entered the neighbor's back yard the man's wife was also there with him turning over the abalone.

"Every two hours we turn them over so they can dry evenly," he explained once we'd been introduced.

Cecil Cheng was George's diving buddy. He was a Chinese American who had been a soldier in the US Army and before the end of the 2nd World War had been stationed in Melbourne. On his free days he had been snorkeling off Cheviot Bay and couldn't believe the abundance of abalone on each rock no matter where he looked. He was able to explore and dive all along the east coast as far up as Sydney. When the war ended, Cecil had to return to the US.

Diving for abalone on the west coast of the US started to become a new industry in the late fifties and early sixties, and the Big Red was the most sought-after ab because of its fine texture and size which was good for abalone steaks. There was even a documentary in *Cinemascope* that was shown in theatres around Melbourne in the late 1950s about diving for abalone in the kelp forests off the coast with people bringing up giant red abalone, shucking them and cooking them on the beach. For many years, canned abalone by Calmex, situated in Ensenada, California, was considered the best.

Cecil had always remembered his time in Australia and when an opportunity presented, he migrated to Australia with his wife and two children, settling in Sydney. When George moved up to Sydney from Melbourne, he happened to buy the house next door to Cecil and his family and they quickly became friends and diving buddies.

Remembering his time before in Australia Cecil started diving for abalone. He dried them and began selling the dried abalone to America at first, and then later, to markets in Hong Kong. Being Chinese was a big advantage for Cecil in opening up a market for his product in Hong Kong.

After we were introduced and George told Cecil that we had a master fishermen's licence, and that we dived for abalone along the south coast, he expressed a desire to buy our abalone in the future. He had recently invested considerable money in establishing a canning factory and had set up a base in Mallacoota. He was also thinking about Phillip Island, much further to the south. We stayed with George and his family for two more days during which, because we couldn't see Zara or her friends who were too busy filming a commercial and doing promotions for the Lido, we managed to organize a means of selling our abalone to Cecil.

Leaving Sydney and heading back to Melbourne, Peter and I decided we would be better off if we had our own boat, so we contacted Fred to tell him what we'd decided, and that he would have to advertise for other divers.

"Don't worry about it," he told us. His doctor had advised him not to go anywhere near abalone or other seafood for that matter, because he suffered severe allergies. "I've got ulcers on my hands and on my arms because of shucking abalone," he said. "I can't go near the things again. I've put my boat up for sale."

He wished us all the best.

Well, that was unexpected to say the least.

Branching out

It took a bit longer than we expected, but by the end of October 1965, Peter and I were ready to branch out on our own, ready for the big dollars, and very excited.

We had purchased 14-foot Savage *tinnie* with a 40 horsepower Evinrude on the back on a single axle trailer from Howard Roberts Marine in

Footscray. The compressor setup was professionally done with the help of Wally, our ex-diving buddy who was a fitter and turner at *Containers*. It was a 6 cubic foot compressor driven by a Briggs and Stratton engine, and the lot was mounted on a stainless-steel frame and bolted on top of the front seat in the boat. Peter built a small reserve tank of stainless-steel with buffers on the inside to separate water from hot air. A pressure gauge was mounted on top, a water tap on the bottom, two charcoal filters were fitted with a T-piece screwed into one of them for our hoses.

A couple of days before we'd completed setting up our dive boat, Les Stephan rang to ask about Fred. I told him we no longer dived for Fred and had set up our own boat. Fred's doctor had advised him to stay away from abalone and fish because of his sever allergic reaction, so he had sold his boat.

"Give us a few more days and we'll be ready to meet you at Cape Everard again."

Checking the compressor... getting ready for Cape Everard.

Early on Thursday the 29th October 1965 with clear blue skies we headed towards Cann River. We stayed the pub where Tom Bidwell had reserved us a room. Cann River was bustling with people who were there for an extended long weekend, since the Tuesday after the weekend was Melbourne Cup Day.

Having dinner with Tom the night we got there, he said, "There's a few divers down from Sydney camped at Cape Everard, so you might find it a bit cramped."

"As long as there's enough room for a tent and our boat, we don't mind."

"Well, no one has dived since you were here last; the weather's been shithouse. There's still a huge swell running so its not safe to get into the water."

That didn't sound too good.

"Maybe you should give Tamboon a try. It's more civilized there with proper camping grounds, showers and a store where you can buy food and other stuff. There's even a new boat ramp."

"That sounds pretty good."

At least there was a decent graded road from Cann River straight down to Tamboon on the coast, and it was no further to drive than Cape Everard.

"You bring whatever abalone you get direct to me and I will pay you an extra three pennies a pound."

"Done," we both said at once.

The next morning, Friday, we drove straight to Tamboon to discover a picturesque little town situated on a beautiful inlet. We went directly to the camping ground and were lucky to get the last double spot to erect our tent beside which we could park our truck and boat.

The weather had improved and everyone at the camp was looking forward to a great weekend.

Over the next couple of days, we put our boat into the water so we could test how it handled as well as try out the compressor and dive a bit to see if everything worked okay. Since it was all new, we had to be sure. We didn't want any of the problems we'd had with Fred and his makeshift gear.

Tuesday was the 3rd of November, Melbourne Cup Day.

We left the camp at 10 am. We had dressed in our wetsuits to save time. We had five large garbage bins in the boat in which we would put the abalone we'd shucked. We were anxious to get out and get to work. At the boat ramp a couple of locals warned us that it was still too dangerous to cross the bar in the harbour to get to the open sea, but from the boat ramp it didn't look that rough.

Were the locals being too cautious?

"Wait another day or two," we were told. "You won't get through in that boat," they said indicating out14-foot tinnie sitting on the boat ramp with Peter ready to back it down into the water.

The water in the inlet was still brown with runoff from the rain we'd had over the last few weeks. No waves, but lots of fine ripples, good for those guys who want to go out and sit in their tinnie with some fishing lines over the side. There were quite a few boats already out.

"Okay, thanks for the advice," I told the guy. "We'll go out and have a look anyway."

Friedrich Glasbrenner

Nothing short of a disaster

We only had to travel about two miles to get to the bar. We passed a lot of boats, but there were only two closer to the bar. Peter was handling the motor and I stood on the bow holding the anchor rope, ready to throw it in if it looked dangerous to proceed. With the tide running out, the water seemed pretty flat. There were some swells out beyond the bar, but they didn't look that big.

"What do you reckon?" Peter yelled over the noise of the outboard.

"It looks pretty flat; we should give it a go."

Peter gunned the motor and we shot towards the bar. But as it got closer, I could see there were some big swells coming in, and where they met the outgoing tide on top of the bar it was churning and splashing, bubbling ferociously. It didn't look good. It looked like water boiling in a kettle. Suddenly we were on top of the bar, in the boiling water. I felt a couple of thumps underneath my feet as the bottom of the boat hit the sand over the bar.

This close to the big swells outside, we could see it was too rough to do any diving so we decided to turn back. We were just over the bar when I saw a huge swell starting to break. The closer it got the bigger it became. I tried to tell Peter to turn into it so we could ride over it, but he'd already started to turn to head back in. The wave was breaking when it hit us. We floated up over the top and as it passed beneath us, we dropped like rock. It was like a ride on the Big Dipper at Luna Park. We flew over the top. We landed hard on the other side. Unfortunately, enough water had got into the boat to stall the engine. As we wallowed in the trough Peter was desperately trying to start the motor again when the next wave started to break over us. I yelled "jump", then dived head first into it. I'd hoped to go under it but it dragged and swirled me along the bottom for a long time. When I finally came up and gulped some air, our boat was upside down and some of our belongings were floating away. Peter's head popped up and he gulped some air. Then another huge wave hit us, and that was the last I saw of him.

This third wave held me down forever. It ripped off part of the rubber sleeve of my wetsuit and as I rolled along in the sand on the bottom I thought, This was it. I was not going to get out this. Had I not been wearing a wetsuit, which is fairly buoyant without lead weights, or been good at snorkeling, I would certainly not have survived. I would not have made it back to the surface.

When I finally did, I looked around and there was no sign of our boat, and worse still, no sign of Peter. As the next wave was almost on me, I dived under it and swam up. I tried to ride it, swim with it back to shore, but the outgoing current dragged me further out to sea.

Beyond the breaking waves was nothing but gigantic swells. Once I'd figured out how to use the swells to push me back towards the shore, I stopped worrying about not surviving, I started instead to worry about Peter. Has he drowned? Was he still alive? What would I tell his wife and children if he hadn't survived?

I kept diving into wave after wave, and the skin inside my wetsuit started chafing from the sand that had got in when I was being dragged along the bottom. We really should have listened to the locals and heeded their advice.

I couldn't keep swimming all the time and had to take arrest, lying on my back as the waves lifted me up and down. All my swimming had not got me any closer to shore, but I had drifted some way along the coast.

Resting and drifting I started to question myself. Was being an abalone diver the right thing to do? Would it be better to remain a bus driver for the rest of my life? We'd lost all our equipment, but that didn't matter when I started to think that I'd also lost my best friend.

I don't know how long I rested on my back but with the sun shining down and the constant wind blowing, my lips started to blister and my tongue seemed swollen. I was very thirsty.

The current had taken me a long way from the bar but I was closer to the shoreline now, and feeling slightly regenerated after the rest, I started swimming, using the waves to give me a bit of a push, towards the shore. As I came up on top of a wave, I saw Peter jumping up and down on the beach. He still had on his wetsuit pants. He waved his arms and yelled something but I couldn't hear the words. But I was excited to see him alive. I'd thought he was dead.

I started swimming with as much strength as I could muster towards the beach. He ran along the beach keeping parallel to me as I swam towards it. It was only a few hundred feet, but it was the hardest I ever had to swim, because the damned current never slackened for one moment. I was swimming sideways across it as it ran parallel to the beach. There was no way I could have swum against it as I tried nearer to the bar, but swimming across it I finally made it to the beach and staggered onto the sand. Peter grabbed and hugged me, and we started dancing around like demented kids.

"I thought you were dead," Peter said.

"I thought you were dead," I told him almost at the same instant.

By the time we'd got over the sand dunes along the beach and were closer to the inlet of the harbour a man in a fishing boat spotted us and came over to give us some water. He told us 'Light Fingers' had won the Melbourne Cup. That meant I'd been in the water from 10-30 am until 3-30 pm, that I'd been swimming for almost five hours. No wonder I was fucking exhausted.

The fisherman gave us ride back to the boat ramp where we'd left the truck. While on the way Peter told me he had jumped into the second wave on the opposite side of the boat from me, and grabbed a pair of flippers, but couldn't get them on before the next wave hit him and dragged him under. When he finally came up, because he was good at surfing, he managed to ride the following wave back to shore.

"When I was trying to start the engine, I saw you dive in. I realized I had to do the same, and that's the last time I saw you. When I came up the current had dragged me along the shoreline and once clear of the bar, I was able to surf my way back to the beach. I started running along the beach looking for you then."

We were probably no more than five hundred feet apart, but because he was closer to shore than I was, he made it back long before I could.

That was a day neither of us will ever forget.

Back at the boat ramp we had to put up with friendly banter about being stupid *squareheads* who had to find out the hard way how dangerous the bar was…

But in the end, they were happy we were alive and everyone wanted to pat us on the back and give us drink. Most of them found it hard to believe that we had survived. According to the locals, the salmon were running and the sea was full of sharks chasing after them.

Eventually, after everyone had heard our story, we managed to get into the shower for a clean up and fell into bed in out tent totally exhausted.

Very early the next morning, a couple of neighbouring campers woke us up to tell us that our boat had been washed ashore on the incoming tide. We jumped up and got dressed and raced down to the boat ramp where some people had turned it over and dragged it up onto the ramp. There was no outboard motor, and no compressor either. The waves had ripped them off. Peter went and got the truck and the trailer and with some help we winched it onto the trailer leaving the boat ramp clear for others to use. On inspecting it, we could hardly believe our luck. There was hardly any damage to the boat itself. The transom where the outboard sat held by clamps was undamaged. But where the compressor was bolted to the front seat, the bolts had been ripped out completely. That was the only real damage, and that, Peter could easily repair.

Not much else to say about that episode other than it certainly put a damper on my plans to be a diver. We packed up our camp and headed home.

A couple of days after we got home Peter decided he wasn't going to be an abalone diver, and insisted that I keep the boat while he would get the insurance on the motor and the compressor. He'd already reapplied and got his old job back as a fitter and turner.

I'd also had a number of calls from Bruce Rogers, the manager of the bus service, asking me to come back to work and "to stop crawling around on the bottom of the sea looking for useless mutton fish."

Once Peter had told me he was going back to work I reluctantly decided to give Bruce a call to tell him I was willing to come back the following week to be a bus driver again.

One more surprise

It happened on Friday morning, on the 12th of November.

The front doorbell was ringing, and when I got up to see who was there, I was surprised to see Harry Humphreys standing there with a huge smile on his face. I had met Harry two years earlier when I had sold my very first abalone haul from the Bay to him, and he'd told me they couldn't really use the Bay abs because the quality wasn't good enough.

"I've got some good news," he said before I even had a chance to say hello.

"Come in then."

I stepped back and by the time we'd walked into the kitchen Zara was there with the kettle on ready to make us a cup of coffee. I introduced Harry to her.

After sipping his coffee Harry said, "Smorgons have leased a fifty-foot steel crayfish boat which they are fitting out to be a dive boat for abalone. It's currently moored at Melbourne Seafoods, in the Maribyrnong River, in Footscray. It's called the Mintak."

Apparently, Smorgons had received some good orders for canned abalone as a result from their earlier experiments, and Harry was overseeing the project for Ray Orloff, one of the CEOs at Smorgons in Somerville Road West Footscray.

"They've advertised for four divers and I've already interviewed three of them. You didn't see the ads?"

Harry Humphreys

"No, I didn't."

"Would you be interested in being the fourth diver? I thought of you while I was doing the last interview, so I figured I'd come around and ask you personally."

"Yes."

"Yes what?"

"Yes, I would be happy to be the fourth diver."

How about that! Harry had come at exactly the right moment. Right when I was thinking of giving up diving, reluctantly, and going back to bus driving. With an opportunity like this, there was no way I would go back to driving a bus. I didn't even have to talk it over with Zara. I looked at her and knew that she understood this is what I wanted to do. She just nodded and smiled.

"I was on my way down to the river to see how things are going, before dropping in here. Do you want to come and have a look at the boat?"

He didn't have to ask me twice.

It was a fifteen-minute drive from my place in North Altona to the industrial area in Footscray, and after passing Safcol, Harry stopped at the wharf outside Melbourne Seafoods, where he introduced me to Ray Orloff, and Les Tuckey, the owner of Melbourne Seafoods and the Mintak.

And there she was, The Mintak, sitting beside the wharf. It looked magnificent sitting there in the Maribyrnong River.

She was all grey except for the wheelhouse which was painted white. I was very excited to go on board because it was the first time I'd ever been on such a magnificent looking boat.

There were several tradesmen working, finishing off bits and pieces.

"She'll be ready in a week," Harry told me as we walked around on deck.

On the way home Harry told me he'd organized a meeting with the other three divers, the skipper and a deckhand which was to take place on board the next day.

"I'll come and get you in the morning," he said as he dropped me off at home.

Going on board the Mintak, Harry led me straight to the wheelhouse where I was introduced to Bob Bush, the captain, Allan, his deckhand who also had a Masters 5 skipper licence which allowed him to skipper a professional fishing boat up to 60 feet long, and the three divers. One of them I was surprised to meet; Billy Smith, a good friend of Peter, my first diving partner. He was there with his cousin Kenney Kittle. There was another smaller fellow from Brisbane who called himself Kenneth Frederick Johnson. He had a very strong handshake and a pleasant smile.

I can't remember how many mugs of coffee we consumed while on board that day, but we got to know each other pretty well and found out each other's life story. We decided to meet again the next day, and by the time Harry took me home, it was late afternoon.

Many years later, Fred and Bob Bush meet again, a joyful reunion.

An idea forms...

Diving with Peter at Cape Everard had been a great time but the only aspect that was difficult was dragging a heavy bag filled with abalone to the surface. I'd been thinking how to get around that ever since then, and over the last few days an idea had slowly formed in my mind. A reverse parachute. A parachute fills with air as a skydiver falls down and slows his descent to earth. What if we had something like a parachute underwater, that you filled with air from your regulator? But instead of falling down, because it was underwater, the air trapped in the chute would lift it up and float to the top. If it was attached to the heavy bag of abalone, you could make it float so you didn't have to drag it over the reef. You could pull it along behind you as you swam along the reef. And when the bag was full of Abs, a bit more air in the canopy would help lift the heavy bag up to the surface.

I couldn't wait to explain all this to Peter, so I called him the moment he got home from work and asked him to meet me at his parent's place. His mother, I recalled, had a sewing machine (a Singer) which was strong enough to sew heavy canvas. I had drawn a rough sketch on a piece of paper of what I thought it might look like.

At his parent's place I explained what I had in mind, and showed them the sketch.

"That's a great idea," Peter said. "I wish we'd had something like that when we were at Cape Everard."

"I think I could sew up something like that, like an open-ended upside-down rucksack," Peter's mother said. "Might take a couple of days though."

"Fantastic," I exclaimed.

"I can make up a fitting for a small air hose you can attach to your lead belt that you can use to inflate it without having to blow air out of your regulator," Peter said.

"Hah! Now we're getting somewhere."

The next few days were a mad rush as I got organized for the long haul. We were to be based at Eden just over the border in NSW, but would work our way south along the Victorian coast. Harry would be there every time the Mintak returned with its load of abalone to transport it to Smorgons for processing. I had to buy a new wetsuit jacket, pants, boots, fins, mask and snorkel and a lead belt, as well as a regulator with appropriate fittings for the air hose. The only dive shop at that time was in Little Lonsdale Street near Exhibition Street.

The rest of the time I spent at the wharf getting to know Les Tuckey and my new colleagues. The Captain Bobby Bush, was a war veteran who had skippered supply boats during the war in New Guinea for the Australian Navy, was retired and lived with his wife Rose in Altona. He told me he was only going to skipper the Mintak until Christmas to make sure Allan learned 'the ropes'. He had bought himself a scallop boat and was going to start dredging in the new year. Billy Smith and Kenny Kittle lived in Maribyrnong and worked at the local Woolstore. Ken Johnson was a Queenslander who had worked as a boner at the abattoirs in Roma, but had wanted a change of scenery. He left that job and was working at a small meatworks in Richmond and shared an apartment with Maurice Parmateer in St Kilda. Being a good snorkeler and having dived with tanks (scuba), when he saw the ad, he immediately got in touch with Smorgons.

The finishing touches with the Mintak progressed rapidly while our excitement grew by the hour.

There were four separate live circulating tanks under the deck, two in front and two behind the wheelhouse, where we could stack live abs in steel crates holding up to 70 or 80 pounds each. Each tank could hold 1000 pounds. On the fore-deck was a 14-foot Savage tinnie with a two and a half horsepower Seagull 2 stroke motor on the back, resting on old tyres, and strapped down firmly.

A large steel frame was mounted at the back of the wheelhouse. It held a big compressor driven by a diesel motor and a huge air tank with lots of filters, water traps and pressure gauges. To top it off there were four rubber hoses, with brass quick-release fittings on each end, would neatly on each side of the frame.

The wheelhouse was relatively small, with doors on each side and a big trapdoor leading to the engine room below. A door through the rear wall led to a comfortable hallway with stairs leading down to the sleeping quarters. There were 5 very comfortable bunks, a couple of storage cupboards, a small shower room and a separate toilet. There was also a small galley and space for eating meals. At the far end of the hall were two bunks, for Bob and Allan the deckhand. There was a ton of room for the six of us.

The Mintak had one single Gardner Diesel engine capable of giving us 8 knots at full speed.

A pat on the back

A couple of days before departure, Peter called and asked me to meet him at his mother's place. The parachute was finished. It looked exactly as I had drawn it. A small upturned backpack with two adjustable straps for a comfortable wear. It was double sewn so the air could not escape easily. Peter bolted a couple of high-pressure air fittings on a lead weight to be worn on the side of my belt. All I had to do was push a button when the potato sac was full and the parachute would lift me and the bag of abalone to the surface. No more hard swimming while trying to lift a heavy weight.

I was rapt, and couldn't thank them enough for the work they had done. "You should give yourself a pat on the back," Peter said. "It's a great idea." I couldn't wait to try it out to see how well it worked.

The arrangement was that after each run, Harry would pick us up and take us back home. Because the abalone was kept alive in the holding tanks, we did not have to shuck them. That would be done at Smorgons. We, the divers, would be paid 5 pence a pound gross weight, but Bob and Allen, the skipper and the deckhand were paid a wage.

Before departure, Harry had taken the four of us to the Department of Fisheries and Game to get ourselves master fishermen's licences. I only had to show my receipt to get mine while the other three had to fork out £1 each.

The Lido was starting a new show in a couple of weeks and Zara was busy with rehearsals. She was happy I was doing something I really wanted to do, so that was good. We didn't have to worry about house repayments because we would have good money coming in.

It was Monday morning of the last week in November when Harry picked me up to take me to the wharf to set sail. It felt great to be on board again. It didn't take long to get settled in. Harry chatted for a while with Allen about communications then wished us well. Waving goodbye to our friends and all the employees at Melbourne Seafoods, we headed south towards Queenscliff where we would stay overnight.

That was my first night's sleep on board a professional fishing boat. As I fell asleep, I felt I was living in a dream.

Approaching a mooring spot for the night at Queenscliff.

A minor setback

Early next morning while Allan topped up the fuel levels so we had a full tank, we had a quick breakfast at a shop onshore. Back on board again, we headed around towards Port Phillip Bay heads and went out through the Rip and into Bass Strait. Now we were really on our way.

There was a strong incoming tide running at 6 knots and it took us a long time to get through the Rip and out into the ocean. Once we were clear we turned east and headed towards Wilson Promontory. We soon passed Phillip Island, Shellback and Norman Islands.

We travelled all day and night, with Bob and Allan swapping places at the helm every four hours. Being able to play chess I was happy to discover Ken also played, and it became a great pastime while on long stretches between diving spots.

As we approached Great Glennie Island in the late afternoon, Bob told us we would anchor in the lee of the island. He thought there might be something wrong with the gearbox and he and Allan wanted to check it in the morning.

Not being a mechanic, I never found out what was wrong, but Bob and Allan spent most of the next day, while we were anchored by the protected side of the island, working in the engine room.

It turned out to be a beautiful day and after breakfast I felt like having a snorkel. The water around the boat was without a ripple and absolutely clear. I put on my bathers, grabbed flippers, mask and snorkel and went down the ladder and into the water. Where we were anchored it was 30 feet deep, stunningly clear, and I dived down to the bottom to have a look. The water, unfortunately, was very cold. I only spent a few moments swimming through kelp while being followed by curious fish before I had to go back up and get out of the water. As soon as I got back on deck Ken handed me a cup of hot coffee, which went down really well because, I had started shivering the moment I came out of the water. The coffee warmed me up.

We sat in the sun, played some chess while Bob and Allan toiled away in the engine room.

It was mid afternoon when they finally emerged from the engine room to inform us that they were almost done, but we would stay here overnight, since it was getting too late to go on. It would be better to start again early in the morning.

Sitting around on the hot deck and feeling far too warm I decided to have another quick snorkel around. This time I swam from the boat towards the edge of the island which was about 20 metres away.

As I snorkeled closer to the island the seaweed changed and there was a lot more fish life. I dived down and almost choked on a mouthful of water when I saw huge abalone on every rock that stretched along the edge of the island. I could hardly believe my eyes. I was so excited to see so many abs I forgot how cold the water was. There were far more abs here than I had seen at Cape Everard.

The guys on board watching me couldn't work out why I stayed so long in the water when it was obviously very cold.

"What's going on?" Ken called out.

I just pointed to the edge of the island and said, "grab a mask and snorkel and swim over to have look." Which they all did.

Bob and Allan came up from the engine room when they heard the commotion we made. They must have thought we were drunk when they saw us dancing about and shaking hands. When we explained why we were so delirious, plans were made to dive right there the next day instead of continuing on to the prom. From what we'd seen, we figured there was enough abalone here to fill all the live tanks without going anywhere else. (Which we did!)

I could hardly sleep that night I was so excited. I wanted to try my parachute to see if it would work as I'd imagined.

By sun-up we were already on deck and could hardly wait to jump into the water. We decided to form two teams, Billy and Kenny plus Ken and me. In later years we were known as Ken and Fred. While we had been having breakfast. Bob and Allen had been busy setting the hoses and the compressor. It was already running when we came up dressed in wetsuits ready to start. It was an enormous feeling of relief on breathing my first breath through the new regulator. It was so clean, almost delicious. So much better than the smelly air we'd used at Cape Everard. There was not a trace of oil fumes or any other impurities.

Ken and I grabbed a sack each and entered the water to start the dive and immediately I had a problem. I couldn't sink. There was a small amount of air trapped in the chute on my back which prevented me from going down. It was like wearing a life vest. It took a moment before I figured that if I dived head first, it would turn the sack upside down and any air trapped would bubble out. I followed Ken down and started working. I couldn't feel the chute on my back but as soon as I filled my sac, I pressed the button to release air into the chute.

I had to remember not to let too much air get in at once or it would drag me up to the surface so quick I could get the bends. I had to remember to ascend slowly. I let a small amount of air dribble into the chute, and immediately felt its buoyancy. It was fabulous to float up to the surface without having to swim hard while hanging onto a sac full of abalone.

Once I'd filled a couple of sacs I got the knack of exactly how much air to release to carry me to the surface. It made working an absolute pleasure rather than a chore. (The chore being having to drag a heavy bag up the surface.)

Since Ken and I were a team I went over to him and said I would swim his full sacs up to the surface so he didn't have to drag them up. I would fill a bag, take it up, come back down and then take up his full bag, then both of us would work our way along the reef filling another sac each, before I repeated the process of floating them up to the surface.

Bob and Allen, on deck, could hardly keep up with the four divers under the water. After only two hours they had filled two of the live holding tanks and were starting on the third one.

One of the sacs Ken handed me to take up had two big crays in it. They would be a beautiful addition to dinner.

It was well before midday when Bob told us to stop. "All the tanks are full. There's nowhere else to put any more."

"That chute of yours," Bob said, "is a marvelous idea. You and Ken have filled a whole tank while Billy and Kenny only managed half a tank."

Because it was so much quicker for us to get a full bag to the surface using the chute, meant we could go back down sooner to start collecting more. That was a huge advantage. Not that it mattered so much here, because the total catch, regardless of how much each diver contributed was to be shared equally. Everything went into the same pot. Naturally I was feeling quite proud of myself for having thought of it. In fact, I was most likely the first diver to think of it.

Bob got onto the two-way radio and contacted Smorgons and told them to bring a truck to Port Welshpool to collect two tons of live abalone.

By the time we had cleaned the deck and stored our gear, Bob had winched up the anchor and we were on our way to Port Welshpool.

We rounded Wilson's Promontory, the most southern point of the Australian mainland, passed the lighthouse, Waterloo Bay, Refuge Cove and Rabbit Island. Allan, in the meantime was boiling three crays, (Billy had also caught one) and being very hungry we devoured them the moment they came out of the pot. There was not a scrap left by the time we reached Port Welshpool.

As dusk descended and we tied up the pier at Port Welshpool the truck from Smorgons was already waiting for us. With all hands on, it only took half an hour to load all the abalone into the truck. The truckie couldn't help smiling as he watched us. He told us she'd never had a load of muttonfish on his meat truck before.

The southern most point of the Australian mainland, Wilson's Promontory, and its lighthouse. Absolutely spectacular when seen from the ocean side.

Tiger abalone. A fine example from the first day of diving.

"Come back in two days' time and we'll have another load ready. Oh, and bring some T-bone steaks when you come back, please," I said.

"No worries, mate."

There was no scale on the truck to weigh the load, but the driver said the weight would be radioed through to us in the morning. He wished us good luck, started his truck and headed back to Melbourne, a long drive. Feeling good, but absolutely stuffed. By the time we had stacked the empty crates on the front deck we retired to our bunks for a good night's sleep.

We were debating how much weight we'd had during breakfast the next morning. Bob was sure we had more than two ton and within an hour Bob had a long conversation with Ray Orloff.

Ray was pleased with the result so far and suggested it might be better to stay based at Port Welshpool instead of going to Eden as the original plan had been. This suited us as well because there was an enormous area that we could dive in, and it was closer to home if for any reason someone had to return. Bob told us we had in total collected 4730 pounds. That was a lot. A rough calculation told us we'd earned £24 each.

That might not sound much these days, but it was quite a lot back in 1965.

And that was only our first real working day, and only half a day at that.

A mess under the pier

While Bob and Allan went to a small store/café/service station to buy some supplies, Billy and I jumped off the pier to have a snorkel around the pylons. Not expecting to find much, because of the number of boats and fishermen that used the pier, we were shocked to discover it was like a garbage dump under the surface. The pier had been there for decades, and like Port Albert, one of the biggest fishing fleets on Victoria's east coast operated out of Port Welshpool.

Everything, and anything you could imagine had been dumped over the side near the pier. There were unrepairable cray pots covered in weed on the bottom, fragments of fishing nets caught on steel plates, fishing rods (dropped or thrown away), bits of broken concrete, cracked and broken bricks, several truck and car tyres, many bottles whole as well as broken; it was almost as if a dump truck had driven along the pier and tipped its load over the side. Yet oddly enough, there was plenty of life under the pier. The pylons were covered with mussels and schools of small fish swam everywhere, and surprisingly, a few good crays hiding under whatever shelter they could find. They most probably had escaped from cray boats while the catch was being unloaded.

I could hardly believe the size of many eels swimming around in search of food. Some of them had to be five feet long. We speared a few because one of the cray fishermen moored near us at the pier asked us, if we were interested to have some eels smoked, he would take them to his brother who had a smokehouse and lived not far from the town. So we shot three and gave them to him.

Fred holding the three eels speared underneath the pier at Port Welshpool. They were rather heavy. Ken's girlfriend Julie came to visit while we were there since Port Welshpool wasn't too far away from Melbourne, and they too posed with the three huge eels.
Even the guys on board had to take turns in holding up the biggest eel for a photo.

The Central Zone

On the Mintak in the background, Kenny is wearing my back pack parachute and is about to go over the side to try it.

The Mintak had caused a small sensation, because it was the first Abalone dive boat in Port Welshpool. While we were moored there for that short time we had a lot of curious people come up and ask us questions.

As soon as Bob and Allan got back with whatever supplies they had bought we didn't waste any time in casting off and heading out, back to the Glennies, and by the time we passed by Rabbit Island, Allan was preparing lunch. We headed right back to the same spot we had earlier dived on, and with plenty of daylight left once we got there, we sorted our gear ready to start diving early the next morning.

Our routine was the same as before, except this time we were faster and by eleven o'clock we had all four holding tanks full plus some spare crates standing on deck also full. While Ken and Billy helped to clean the deck, Kenny and I stayed in the water and caught some more crays as well as spearing a dozen different fish.

Once the holding tanks were full again, we headed back to Port Welshpool where the truck to take our catch to Melbourne would be waiting.

Kenny Kittle and Fred with some crayfish caught in between diving for abalone.

The truck pulled up and drove onto the pier about the same time as we finished tying up to the pier. To our surprise, Ray Orloff jumped out of the passenger side to greet us like long-lost friends. He shook hands with all of us, but we left it to Bob to answer all his questions while we helped to load the truck. Ray was impressed with the quality of the abs and couldn't stop thanking us enough. We put a couple of crays in the crates as well as some of the fish we'd speared for him to take back home.

Suddenly he was apologizing because he'd forgotten the steaks we'd asked for. "They'll be on the truck next time, in two days when it comes back."

After breakfast the next morning I walked over to the store to phone Zara. I wanted to tell her that we'd changed plans and were staying down at the prom. She said Harry had called, only a few moments earlier, and he was worried about them. He thought something awful must have happened. He was waiting at Eden for us to appear and we hadn't turned up. No one had thought to tell him we'd changed plans.

It took me a while to get out of the store after the phone call because everyone who saw me wanted to talk about the Mintak and the abalone diving. Someone handed me a cup of coffee and of course I was obliged to answer all their questions.

By the time I got back to the Mintak, Bob had already spoken with Ray and was informed that our weight was nearly 3 ton, to be precise 6620 pounds. Just under £35 for each of us.

On the third day of diving, we anchored a couple of hose lengths away from our previous spot and filled our holding tanks plus 8 extra crates before midday. Our teamwork was perfect. Back to Port Welshpool, and just as we had finished loading the abs out of the holding tanks into the crates and stacking them on the deck, the truck pulled up to take the load. A smiling Harry hopped out of the passenger side and could hardly believe his eyes when he saw all the crates of abalone stacked on the deck.

It's easy now to forget that mobile phones never existed back then, had hardly even been imagined. There was only the landline, and no had thought to ring Harry while he waited for us at Eden. When he finally called Ray, he was told that we were working out of Port Welshpool, so he drove back to Melbourne and hitched a ride on the truck coming to collect the abs.

He was over the moon when he found out that stopping to fix the gearbox had resulted in us finding a bonanza. Before we started to load the truck, Jim the driver handed us a bin full of beautiful T-bone steaks. There were eighteen of them. "With regards from Ray," he said with huge grin.

Harry told us that with Christmas coming up soon, we could only do two more trips because Smorgons closed down for the Christmas break. They would start working again on the 4th of January (1966)

"I'll come back and take you back to Melbourne after the last trip. Maybe next year I can join you for a trip or two."

"You're very welcome," we told him.

We gave him and Jim as well, a few crays to take back with them.

Back on board we got stuck into the juicy T-bones for dinner.

Our tally that day was 7500 pounds. It was getting better every time. £39 each. As soon as we'd made our usual phone calls home, we took off early. We planned to catch some crayfish and shoot a few nice fish to take home for Christmas, before nightfall, which we did.

The next morning, we were early in the water, as soon as the sun came up and we worked like demons. We were finished by midday, and we had outdone ourselves again. When we got back, we had 8800 pounds. £45 each.

Harry had asked us to make it a shorter day the last day because it would take quite some time to get us home.

On our last trip out for the year we did the same as we'd done the first time. We knocked off at 10 am, after filling two holding tanks with abalone and one with a few crays and some fish to give to people as presents, and headed back to Port Welshpool, tying up around 7 pm. The truck pulled up

The Central Zone

a few minutes later, followed by Harry in his Holden station wagon.

It didn't take too long to offload because on the way back we had packed all our gear and made the Mintak spic and span. Bob and Allan travelled in the truck, and the four of us divers were in the station wagon with Harry. It was Monday the 20th of December and Harry told us that we would all meet at Smorgons on the Wednesday, when we would get our cash as well as have a Christmas party.

Just as we were securing the Mintak for the time we would be away, the fisherman I'd spoken to earlier, whom I given the ells, turned up and presented us with some beautifully smoked pieces of eel. That was an unexpected treat.

By the time I got home, I was stuffed, so tired I could hardly keep my eyes open, when the front door opened and Zara rushed out to give me a huge welcoming hug. With her arms around me, I couldn't help thinking "Life is so great."

Most of our family and friends and some neighbours turned up the next day wanting to hear all about our adventures. In between harry phoned to tell me that our weight was 5840 pounds and told us he would pick us up at 11 o'clock to take us to Smorgons.

It was nice to catch up with Ray and to meet his wife. Bob and his wife Rose were there also Les Tuckey and son. Ken had just arrived and introduced us to his lovely girlfriend Julie. Allan, Bill and Kenny arrived shortly after. A staff member filled glasses with champagne which Ray handed to each of us. We toasted Christmas and the new year wishing each other all the success possible. Shortly after that we adjourned to a larger room where a long table was covered with lots of goodies to eat.

It was a wonderful afternoon, especially when Ray handed each of us an envelope with our earnings. The only sad moment was when we had to say goodbye to Bob who would be starting his own new adventure in the new year. We wished all the best.

We invited Ken and Julie to follow us home for a few drinks for Christmas. The moment we got home we couldn't resist opening the envelopes which had been burning a hole in our pockets. We were surprised to find £180 in cash, more than we had expected. That meant in less than three weeks I had earned more than I would have on the buses in three months. Wow!

The next few days were hectic with Ken visiting us every day. I introduced him to Zara's family who only lived 10 minutes away and they invited him and Julie to have Christmas dinner with the family. He was most impressed with their generosity.

He also wanted to meet Peter's mother to see if he could get her to make him a parachute like she'd made for me.

Because Christmas day fell on a Saturday, the Tuesday after Boxing Day was a public holiday.

At the Smorgons Christmas party Harry had invited us to meet him at a pub in Footscray which we did, to work out a plan, if we were still willing to dive before the New Year. We were all there except for Bob Bush. Harry had suggested to us, along with Allan, that we could start early and dive some of the islands around the Prom before the New Year started. Of course, we were all interested. We would start 1966 on new reefs.

After lunch the next day, Harry picked Ken and me up to take us to the Mintak. Bill and Allen followed us in Kenny's holden. Driving through Dandenong, Cranbourne, Koo Wee Rup Korumburra, Leongatha, Foster to Weslshpool took close to four hours.

Today, with new highways and better roads it only takes half that time.

It felt great to jump on board again and after a good clean-up it didn't take long to get settled in. Harry chatted with Allen for a while about communications, then wished us well before leaving, and then we were on our own again.

Early the next morning Allan refueled the Mintak with diesel and topped up our water tanks, and after a quick breakfast at the store onshore we were on our way again.

We didn't go as far as the Glennies because we wanted to explore Anser Island and on the way, to have a dive at the mainland under the lighthouse. Bill and Kenny put on their gear, jumped into the water, and in less than 15 minutes later, resurfaced with a full bag each. They were full of smiles.

"There's abalone everywhere," they told us. "And lots of big fish too. Give us a couple more bags."

I tossed the bags over and they disappeared under the water, again returning quickly with the bags full.

It was not very safe to keep the Mintak there so the guys came back on board and we moved across to Anser Island where we anchored in its lee. Ken and I naturally could hardly wait to get back into the water, but once over the side we were a disappointed. There was no bonanza like there had been at the Glennies, and it took quite a while before we were able to fill our bags.

This time it was hard work, and not as much fun as it had been a few weeks earlier. We shifted the Mintak a couple of times and did a fair bit of swimming. We did come across several patches of good sized Green-lip abalone as well as black lip, plus we grabbed five crays.

The Central Zone

Black lip and tiger lip abalone mixed together on the deck. We separated them into different bins.

A beautiful green-lip abalone.

Kenny holding one of the crays we had later for dinner.

It was late afternoon when Ken and I finally got out of the water and to our surprise we had more greens than blacks. We decided to keep them in separate tanks.

Friday was the last day of 1965. It was a brilliant day, with a deep blue sky, and the ocean flat as far as you could see. We decided to check out some spots on the mainland close to Tidal River, because we wanted to anchor in Oberon Bay for New Year's Eve. It was a well-known safe anchorage.

During the day we dived at several spots and charted some of the better ones for future reference. Allan also cooked the crays. By the time we anchored we had a full tank of blacks and half a tank of greens, plus a few more crayfish.

It was still daylight and very warm when this beautiful 60-foot yacht sailed into the bay and anchored not far from us. Several of the crew waved to us. One of the fellows called out and asked if we'd like to join them in celebrating the New year.

Well. He didn't have to ask twice.

As night fell, we had the seagull outboard mounted on our tinny in the water and as the moon came up, Allan motored us across to the yacht and we tied up at the back of the platform. We were welcomed by six smartly dressed young guys in shorts and short-sleeved shirts with the Sandringham Yacht Club emblem on their right sleeve. We handed them several cooked crays as a gift, and were showered in return with all kinds of drinks and invited to partake of the goodies laid out on a large table in a beautifully elegant dining area. I had never seen such a luxurious yacht before. It was like something that belonged to a millionaire, the kind of luxury yacht you see in the movies moored at some place like Monte Carlo. And here we were, a bunch of abalone divers dressed in whatever 'scruffy' gear we had, enjoying such luxury. Needless to say, were all a bit drunk, a bit under the weather when midnight arrived to herald in the New Year.

Over the years, as I celebrated many New Year's Eves, I always remember that night in Oberon Bay. I think of those guys who had sailed along the Victorian coast on a long weekend, not expecting to celebrate New Year's Eve with a bunch of fishermen. We had such a great time.

At 2 am we climbed down into our tinny to return to the Mintak. Not surprisingly, Allan couldn't start the motor, and we had to paddle back to our boat. We didn't have any oars, so we each leaned over the side and used our hands as paddles, while loud music emanated from the Yacht, *Santa Luchia,* which could probably be heard as far away as Tidal River. We sang along with the music as we paddled.

It was dark and we could hardly see the Mintak. It was nothing more than a shadow outlined against a sky full of brilliant starts. If it hadn't been for the full moon, we probably wouldn't have seen it and may have got lost. As drunk as we were, when we tied up alongside the Mintak, we all managed to climb back on board without falling into the sea.

New Year's Day; it was close to midday when we emerged from our bunks, suffering to various degrees, the effects of too much good cheer the night before. Allan jumped down into the tinnie and had no trouble starting the outboard motor this time. He motored across to the yacht and picked up a couple of the guys who had expressed an interest in our activities. He brought them on board, and we all joked about our hangovers. We then showed them over the Mintak, so they could see the holding tanks with the live abalone, our diving gear and whatever else they seemed interested in. After Allan ferried them back to their yacht, they shortly after set sail. As they left the harbour, we wondered if we would ever see them again.

The rest of the day we spent drinking lots of coffee, and fresh water, to get rid of our hangovers.

By the time we anchored again at Anser Island, we had two full tanks of blacklip abalone and one of greenlip abalone, knowing we only had to dive for a couple of hours to fill the last tank.

Allan got in touch with Harry and told him we would have a good load the next evening.

We were in the water by 9 am and three hours later we had to stop diving, because Allan couldn't keep up with four divers sending him bag after bag full of top-class abalone. He had filled the last tank, along with several crates.

Two of the fantastic locations where we dived around the Wilson Promontory area.

The Central Zone

Reefs near Kanowna Island at the Prom. A great spot for green-lips

The last few bags he left stacked against the side of the wheelhouse, while he got ready to pull up the anchor. We stacked the abs into the remaining bins while Allan set course for Port Welshpool.

By the time we tied up at the pier it was dusk, and the truck had been waiting for over an hour. We got stuck into transferring the abs into the truck and it was completely dark by the time we'd finished. We were also exhausted, but excited at the same time. It looked like this was our biggest load ever.

We decided, since we were there, we would explore some of the islands around Wilson's Promontory. We dived at Rabbit Island and The Cliffies, West and East Moncur, Rodondo, and Kanowna.

We went as far as Deal Island, diving often with seals. We had some fantastic dives in crystal clear water, and some deep dives as well. We were very careful on the deeper dives to take enough time to decompress, so we wouldn't get the bends.

Divers like abalone divers, who spend a lot of time underwater, even though in many cases it is only shallow, the time spent underwater breathing compressed air will still cause nitrogen to dissolve in the blood. If the diver surfaces too fast, there isn't enough time for the dissolved nitrogen to exit the blood stream, and it could form tiny gas bubbles that lodge in the joints like the shoulders and in other areas causing severe problems. The quicker you come up, the quicker the gas bubbles expand in the blood, so abalone divers try to take a fair bit of time returning to the surface to avoid the nitrogen bubbling.

Everywhere we dived, we found some good patches of abalone, so naturally we collected as much as we could and never came back without our holding tanks full. We had to pick good weather for our diving, so we listened to the local cray and net fishermen who knew the area because many of them had lived and worked there their whole lives. When the weather was bad, we would return to Melbourne in Kenny's Station Wagon to visit our families, catch up with our washing before getting ready for the next dive trip.

When February (1966) started Australia switched to decimal currency and from then on, we got paid in cents and dollars instead of pounds, shillings and pence. Everything was still weighed in pounds instead of kilos which was a bit confusing at first, but we soon got used to it. Like everyone else, we had to. Eventually the weights became decimal as well. Not only that, we now travelled kilometres instead of miles, although a nautical mile, which is slightly longer than a mile measured on land, stayed the same.

A couple of weeks later Harry informed us that by the first of April (1966) the lease on the Mintak would expire, and we had to bring the boat back to Melbourne Seafoods. Apparently, Les Tuckey had decided to fit the boat out with two new diesel motors and was going to use it first as a charter dive boat, and if that didn't work, he would refit it so he could trawl for scallops.

That was a bit of a bummer. We had gotten used to working and diving for abalone with the Mintak. We would certainly miss our special boat.

But to cheer us up, Harry told us that Smorgons and a couple of other companies had decided they would buy shucked abalone from Port Phillip Bay. The price wasn't as good, but before they weren't willing to buy it at all; now they were.

We made the best of the time we had left getting to know the best dive spots at Wilson's Promontory and its nearby islands. We anchored at Refuge Cove, Waterloo Bay, and Sealers Cove. At refuge cove, during the last week we had before we had to return the boat, we even encouraged Allan to have a go at diving using the compressor. We nearly drowned the poor fellow. How would it have looked, skippering the Mintak back with a dead skipper on board?

We were all feeling sad as we returned the Mintak to its mooring in the Maribyrnong River in Footscray. It had been home to all of us for long enough that none would ever forget the time spent on board.

Allan, our Skipper, about to try diving for the first time. Kenny is watching him.

Ken and Fred in Port Phillip Bay off Williamstown Back Beach, getting ready to start work. Fred is wearing his backpack parachute. Note the old style aqualung regulator that Ken is using.

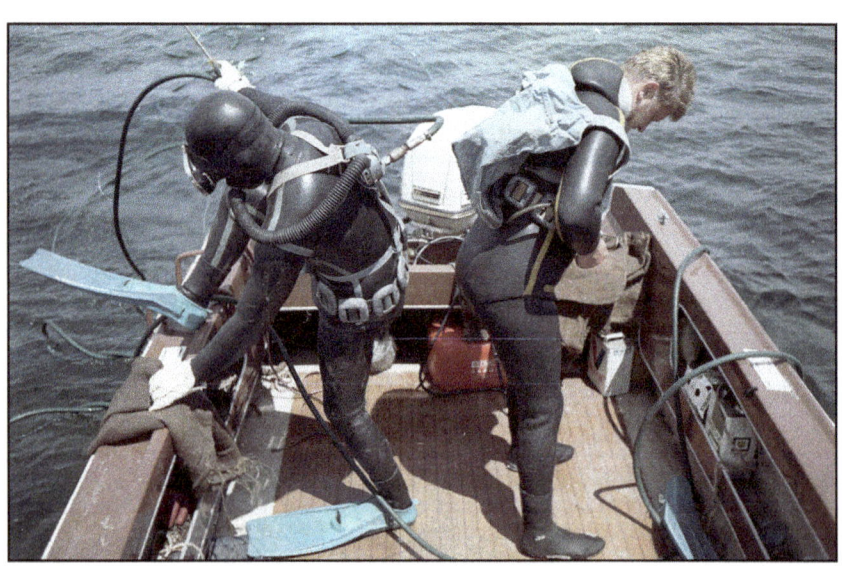

The Central Zone

Part Two
Port Phillip Bay

Fred and Ken with their shared tinny at Williamstown Back beach.

We made a great team

Fred and Ken, or Ken and Fred; whichever way you looked at it, we made a good team working together on the Mintak and we decided to stay together as a team. We both lived in Melbourne, so the logical place to dive was Port Phillip Bay.

It was April, and the weather in Melbourne was fabulous, which was great for diving in the Bay, but we had no equipment except for my 14-foot Savage tinny, plus our wetsuits, fins, masks and snorkels. We had decided we were going to try snorkeling for abs in the Bay off the Williamstown Back Beach. We asked Les Tuckey if we could borrow the Seagull outboard motor, plus a couple garbage bins.

"Sure, not a problem," he assured us, "as long as you sell the abs to me."

"We're happy to do that."

Ken had a Holden car with a tow bar, so we could pull and launch the tinny. Zara and I both had VW Beetles which were useless for towing a boat. They were great little cars though.

Off we went. We got the boat into the water and went out near the old Gellibrand lighthouse where we had first dived for abalone some time back. It was hard work. Using a compressor had made us lazy. We only managed a few abs at a time before having to come up for air. We would dump the abs in the boat and go down for a few more. Fortunately, the water was not very deep on the reefs between the lighthouse and the rocky back beach. We seemed to have collected a lot of Abs but on shucking the flesh from the shell, it wasn't that much. It weighed in at 30 pounds or around 15 kilos. We got paid $4-50 in cash. We did this for several days, moving along the reefs close to shore and each day our haul was a bit better.

We couldn't help noticing more and more boats of all kinds, with two or three snorkelers on board diving for Abs just like we were. We also noticed that a few boats had small compressors on board which of course gave their diver a big advantage, in not having to come up for air every minute or so. Being able to stay on the bottom was so much less tiring and all the time wasted swimming up and down could be used to collect more Abs.

After talking to Peter about this he came to our rescue with a small Tuffy compressor from his workshop. It was mounted on a square piece of marine plywood, and driven by a small 2-stroke motor that made a hell of a noise. Peter had welded a T-piece to the outlet for two short hoses, with a quick-release fitting on either end for our regulators. Because there weren't any filters it had a long exhaust pipe to keep the fumes from the motor away. We clamped the compressor on its base board to the front seat.

We had a couple of steel hooks hanging on each side of the boat so we could hang our full sacks there. It needed the two of us in the boat to lift them on board. Out on the water, we started the compressor, grabbed our gear and dropped over the side. The air tasted bad, and we couldn't work for more than two hours. When we came up we had splitting headaches. When we finished shucking the Abs, we had 110 pounds (a bit over 50 kilos).

We put up with the Tuffy for a few days, until the weather changed. We went and talked to Les again and asked him if he could help us with a new compressor and a Briggs and Stratton engine to power it. He immediately went and asked his secretary to write out an order for what we had asked, and came back and told us they would take 2 cents a pound (4 cents a kilo) from our catch until it was paid off. We considered ourselves lucky to know someone like him.

Peter and Wally did the set-up for us in Peter's workshop, and after several days we had a professional outfit and were ready to do some serious work. We had 150 feet of reinforced water hose each, which gave us a big half circle on each side of the boat to work in. It was very seldom that we came across each other underwater.

Quite often the Seagull wouldn't start. We had to leave the compressor running, dive down to the anchor and pull the boat by swimming along the bottom.

Sometimes, our Briggs and Stratton stopped because it ran out of fuel. As soon as we felt we were running out of air, we would swim up to the surface. Whoever hit the surface first had to swim back to the boat, refuel the compressor motor and start it again.

For a long time, we launched at Williamstown, but it was very difficult at low tide. There was a small channel between the reef that the local amateur fishing club members used, but there was no ramp. There was an ancient wooden boat ramp next to Gem Pier in Nelson Place, but we didn't want to chance it with our unreliable Seagull outboard.

We had to tow our load still inside the boat on the trailer behind Ken's Holden to Melbourne Seafoods, until we ran into Bob Bush unloading his scallops at the pier. He offered us his 20-year-old Dodge Fargo for $20 which was perfect for us. This meant that we could take our catch on the boat home, and then deliver it in the old Ute.

Initially we were happy with what we got at the Back Beach, but we found out there were reefs all the way from Altona across to Point Cook and beyond so we started to launch our tinny at Altona to work those reefs. Whenever we managed to launch easily at high tide in Altona, we inevitably had difficulty when we came back because it would be low tide and there was a lot of mud and sloppy sand that made getting a boat in or out of the water extremely difficult.

We decided we needed a better more reliable outboard motor and went to see the dealer closest to us. Howard Roberts Marine in Victoria Street Footscray. (Howard lived in Williamstown and became a lifelong friend.) A few days earlier someone had needed a bigger outboard and had traded in a 40 horsepower Evinrude, the same model as the one Peter and I lost at Tamboon. Howard offered it to us for the trade-in price, and said he would service it and mount it free of charge. It was a good deal.

We took the Seagull back to Les Tuckey and asked him if he would finance the outboard, and without a blink of an eye, we had another order form written out by his secretary. After that we started using the old ramp at Gem Pier. Rounding the breakwater, past the lighthouse, we often went to the crystal pool first, and then on to Altona. Everything was so much easier when you had good equipment.

As time went on, we encountered many more boats, some with as many as six divers on board, all trying to make easy money. It became extremely annoying when they anchored close to us and we could see them underwater taking 'our' Abs. We had plenty of arguments with them, but all they told us was to "Get stuffed." Most of them had no licence and their boats weren't registered commercially.

I suppose if it hadn't been in the middle of winter with the water extremely cold, there would probably have been a lot more of them. We wore woolen socks on our feet and garden gloves for handling the Abs, but often we would suffer severe headaches because of the coldness of the water. Even wetsuits after a few hours in the water didn't keep us warm and we would emerge frozen stiff, and still had to shuck the abs and then deliver them.

I remember getting home and having to get Zara to help me out of the wetsuit so I could take a hot shower. She was stunned to see I was blue all over, and couldn't stop shivering.

Even though it was cold during the winter months, the visibility was great and we were able to dive four, sometimes five days a week, and we were always happy if we did better than the previous week. With the compressor running, we towed each other underwater, searching for new reefs. We did well after we came across the 'sand dunes' in Altona Bay and eventually Point Cook.

Keeping an eye on the weather was important, because it could change very quickly while were diving. The bay between Point Cook and Williamstown could get very choppy and rough, almost within minutes, and that made it difficult if we had a full load. A couple of times when we got caught in a sudden change, we thought we would be swamped, that we would not only lose the catch but our boat as well. There's a huge area of water surface in the Bay that the wind can blow across, and that allows for some very large but broken waves, quite dangerous for a small heavily laden boat.

By October the water temperature started to rise. We enjoyed the warmer water, but with relentless south and south-westerlies blowing, we couldn't take the chance of driving as far as Point Cook, so we had to stick close to Williamstown and Altona where we got smaller catches.

By November the cost of our fishing licences went up by $2, also our boat registration fee.

Les Tuckey closed his factory over the Christmas and New Year so we took a break. I remember around mid-January I bumped into Greek fisherman and he told me that he always caught some 'mutton fish' in his nets when he fished off Kirk's Point, near Werribee. "You wouldn't have any trouble getting your boat in the water there," he told me. His boat was around the same size as ours and he always went in without a problem.

As soon as Les Tuckey re-opened for the new year, Ken and I went straight to the 'shitfarm' (we called it that because Kirk's Point was not far from the sewerage plant at Werribee, which serviced the Melbourne metropolitan area). It was a bit hard pushing our boat into the water off the sand, especially at low tide, but we managed, and soon discovered a bonanza in only five feet of water. We had to be careful not to hit some of the shallow reefs with our boat, as we worked our way around the reefs.

Every rock was covered with abalone, two or three of them stacked on top of each other, and we filled sack after sack in record time. We would leave each filled sack underneath the boat until we ran out of sacks, then we hauled them up into the boat. We worked for a couple of hours and would have broken our previous records if we didn't have to stop and take the time to shuck the abs in the boat. If we just returned with the sacks full the sheer weight of abalone in the shells would have been too heavy for us to get the boat out of the water and onto the beach. Shucking the abalone in the boat, placing the meat into the bins we had on board, and throwing the shells and guts over the side reduced the weight enough for us to get the boat back to the water's edge where Ken backed our Ute with the trailer down into the water.

We lifted the bins of abalone from the boat and onto the back of the Ute. Hauled the boat up onto the trailer, and we were good to go. We'd filled six garbage bins with top quality shucked abalone, and couldn't be happier. Absolutely exhausted, because it was hard work, but ecstatic at the same time for having completed such a successful day's work.

Ken and I had Kirk's point to ourselves for several months before some of the Ocean divers started to dive in the bay. We started coming across more and more dive-boats, some registered, but the majority unregistered and therefore illegal. Even Ken's roommate Maurice Parmateer bought himself a 16-foot Savage fibreglass Riviera with an 80 HP Johnson Outboard after he found out the Ken earned more than he did at the meat-works. We helped him to fit it out with the latest dive gear. Maurice wasn't short of a quid, but he couldn't dive so he hired a couple of young blokes who'd done some scuba diving and offered them a percentage of whatever the catch was.

By this time, John Strow had opened Vic. Canneries in Northcote and bought Bay abalone. So did Ocean Gardens, South Pacific Canneries in Collingwood, plus Russell Crayfish in Richmond. There were more places than ever where you could sell abalone.

Over a couple of weeks, Ken's roommate Maurice sold several bins of Ab meat to Les Tuckey, but was eventually told not to bring any more, because the meat was of such poor quality it couldn't be sold as third grade. More often than not it was undersized, badly ripped off the reef and had been shucked incorrectly causing further damage to the meat. Because we had asked Les Tuckey to buy Maurice's Abs, and we didn't want our name blemished, we asked Maurice to sell his Abs to Russell Crayfish. We had seen some of Maurice's Ab meat and after meeting his divers we concluded that they wouldn't last too long. Having dived on the Mintak, Ken and I had mastered the ability to recognize the right size and whether the individual abalone was well nourished. We were very selective and only harvested the best. Whereas these amateurs, took anything they could see, no matter what the size or the quality.

According to the fisheries, at that time, they had issued over 400 Master Fishermen's licences, which became a problem for us because we knew there were just as many unlicensed people diving for Abs. With all those divers, the reefs were rapidly being depleted.

By the end of May 1967, Maurice ran out of canneries who would take his abalone, and also his divers didn't want to work in the colder water that would fill the Bay during winter.

On a cold morning Ken surprised me with the news that Maurice wanted to sell his boat.

"We should buy it," he said. "Maurice has had enough. He's already gone back to the meat-works."

When Ken told me how much Maurice wanted, I agreed immediately and we went and spoke to Les Tuckey about it. He immediately forwarded the money to Maurice, and now we had a 16-foot fibreglass Riviera.

We only used our tinny twice at Kirk's Point, while Peter and Wally checked out our new acquisition for a few days to make sure it was all in order. From then on, we launched at the boat ramp beside Gem pier and could travel all over the Bay.

Ken and Fred with a full load of abalone in their new Riviera.

It was around this time we met Thomas (Tommy) Ryan from Torquay and his deckhand David Snelling. They mainly dived for green-lip abalone in the ocean off Torquay, but when the ocean was rough, they came into the Bay. We found them a couple of times off Point Cook and at Kirk's Point, as well as at the Williamstown Back Beach. We became good friends.

When Tommy found out we still had our tinny, he invited us to come to Torquay and dive for green-lips using the tinny. Being light, and not as big as our current boat, the tinny would be easy to launch directly from the beach. "I'll show you some good spots," he told us. And he certainly did.

Fred with Tommy Ryan and Dave Snelling at Williamstown back beach.

A totally different ball game

Working out of our Riviera was a totally different ball game, with launching at the boat ramp in Williamstown so much easier. Getting back into the boat was breeze because Peter had made us a portable ladder which meant we didn't have to climb back up next to the outboard. It also helped considerably with the lifting of the full sacks into the boat. The only drawback was shelling the abs after we'd finished diving, until Les Tuckey suggested we should deliver our catch in the shell and offered us 8 cents a pound, (less 2 cents to pay back our loan).

That was a great relief because it enabled us to have so much more diving time, so we could collect more. It also allowed us to take the abs we'd collected directly by boat up the Maribyrnong River to unload and weigh our catch at Melbourne Seafoods Fishermen's Wharf. No more transferring the catch to the Ute and driving to Footscray. Once unloaded at the wharf we drove the boat back to the boat ramp. It made everything so much better.

We set ourselves a goal of filling ten 50-pound sacks each, but kept going if we were on a good spot. We worked well together with myself on one side of the boat and Ken on the other. With a 150-foot-long hose each, we rarely came across each other, because we kept to our own side of the boat, unless one side had more or better abs, then we would both work the same side together.

One day at Kirk's point, we bumped into Tommy again and he invited us to come to his place in Torquay in a few days because the weather looked like it was going to be good, and we would get some good days for diving.

Tommy with his wife Paula and their two young sons lived in a big weatherboard house in Grossman's Road Torquay. They made us very welcome when we arrived early one fine morning. We had no problems launching our boats off the beach in front of the Life Saving Club and followed Tommy and Dave about a quarter of a mile straight out from the land. We anchored at a spot where Tommy indicated we would have good diving. He warned us to be careful, to make sure we decompressed when we wanted to come up, because we would be diving at a depth of around 60 feet.

On Tommy's advice, a few days earlier Peter had cut us two shorter hoses with a T piece on the end, which connected to the main hose. That meant the two of us were diving off the one hose but close together so we could keep an eye on each other.

We grabbed a sack each and jumped into the unknown.

Getting into the water, we couldn't see the bottom so we followed the anchor rope down, equalizing several times before we got to the bottom.

Tommy had certainly picked a good spot for us to anchor. We were over a large sandstone reef and there was a lot of sea life. But most importantly, the reef was covered with greens everywhere.

Diving for greenlip abalone out here was different to what we were used to from The Prom or diving in the Bay. The greens seemed to prefer an open sandstone bottom to graze on. They also clustered around the bottoms of large volcanic boulders. Nearly all the big ones we saw had weed growing on the back of their shells. Filling our sacks was the easy part and didn't take longer than twenty minutes, but getting them back to the surface took all our strength, especially mine. Without my parachute on my back, it would have been near impossible. I also had to remember to go slow and to stop and hover a couple of times to allow for decompression. So naturally, I followed the anchor rope back up to the boat. Ken came up beside me and being the lighter one, he climbed into the boat to help haul the sack up out of the water. We did this six times before we stopped and started shelling, to finish up with a couple of bins full of meat. When we were finished, we followed Tommy back to shore.

Back at Tommy's place Paula greeted us with a cup of hot tea and a couple of sandwiches. After that we loaded our catch into the Ute and followed Tommy to Geelong where we sold our Abs to Blackney Seafoods. They paid us 55cents a pound which gave us $115. Tommy, because he had a deckhand, had twice as much as us. But we were delighted.

We managed three and half good diving days, but by midday on the last day we got hit by a southerly buster, which wasn't good for our little tinny. We finished up with $450 for the run and were very happy with that. We told Tommy that next time, we would bring our Riviera, because for $5 a guy from the Life Saving Club could launch our boat using his tractor to drive across the sand.

Our Riviera gave us heaps of opportunities to dive in the Bay because we could work which ever way the wind was blowing. With northerlies blowing we could work Williamstown and Altona. With easterlies, Port Melbourne as far as Rickett's Point. With westerlies and southerlies, we worked from Point Cook, She Oak to Kirk's Point.

New Suits

One very cold morning Tommy pulled up next to us as we were getting ready to start working at Kirk's Point.

"Hey guys," he called out. "Have a look at this."

He was wearing a brand new wetsuit. I hadn't seen one like that before.

"Check out my Calypso wetsuit."

He immediately jumped into the freezing Bay water and swam around our boat a couple of times.

"It's like swimming in a heated pool," he said as he climbed on board so we could see it up close.

It was a two-piece suit with a hood to keep the cold water from giving you a headache. It was lined with a soft almost fleecy material on the inside. The bottom half came all the way up to the shoulders, (like a skin tight overall), while the top half with the hood came all the way down to the groin, giving you a double layer from the groin to the chest to keep you extra warm. He also had boots made of the same material for the feet.

"It was designed by Cousteau," Tommy said.

And that was it; once he said Cousteau. Jacques Yves Cousteau was one of our heroes. A diver and inventor, he was a genius, and we were most impressed with the suit Tommy showed us. We would be ordering a suit just like it as soon as we got back to shore.

At that time, we were still wearing three-piece wetsuits, with the legs coming up to the waist, the top half coming down to the groin, and a separate hood if you needed it. Often cold water would run down your back. And not one part of it was fleecy lined. It was just bare sponge rubber. We had to add socks to keep our feet warm. Better than nothing, it was barely adequate; but for a long time, it was all you could get.

As soon as we returned from our day's diving we went to our nearest dive shop and ordered a new Calypso suit each. We were told it would be at least two weeks before we could get them. It took three weeks, and what a difference the new suits made. Because we stayed so much warmer we could last longer in the water, and that extra couple of hours allowed us to increase our catch dramatically.

Unexpected changes

By the end of 1967 we had several runs of good weather at Torquay. Tommy and Paula offered to let us stay with them so we got more time in the ocean. We also had to renew our Master Fishermen's licence which cost $4, which had been changed to an abalone diver's licence, but word was that it would go up within the next twelve months, and that it would go as high as $200. That was a huge jump which at the time we couldn't believe.

One of Tommy's mates offered to be our deckhand and sheller. He had worked with other divers and knew where some good reefs were located. His help eliminated a couple of problems. First, we didn't have to be tied together via the T-piece, and could work separately because we had someone on board who could monitor our compressor and keep an eye on our bubbles in the water. Second; he would help get the sacks into boat, and do the shelling which gave us more time underwater to collect more abalone. And thirdly, he knew the exact spots where some very good reefs were, which saved a lot of time looking.

In the ocean I used my parachute to help lift the sacks back to the surface. I didn't need to do this in the Bay because it was generally quite shallow. But we were in much deeper water in the ocean and using the parachute was essential.

In the Bay we worked without a deckhand because we didn't have to shell the abalone, and just before the Christmas break, we made our last payment to Les Tuckey. It was a huge relief, to be free of debt.

As we entered the new year, 1968, we could still dive all over Victoria and NSW, but half way through the year (1968) the Victorian government changed the laws and established three commercial fishing zones: East, Central, and Western. East was from the NSW border to Lakes Entrance. Central was from Lakes Entrance along the coast to Hopkins River, Warrnambool, and West was from Warrnambool to the SA border. Size limits were established, and the Fisheries and Games Dept would issue large fines for anyone caught taking undersized abalone.

We were also told that our Master Fisherman's licence would go up to $200 annually starting from September 1968. And to maintain that licence, 75% of income had to be derived from some form of fishing, or from working within the fishing industry.

The rumors were right. It was a big jump, and nobody was happy about it, but to stay in the business we had to pay it. That's all there was to it.

Up until that point, we could have dived anywhere along the Victorian coast, but once zones were established, we had to select which zone we wanted to work, so living in Melbourne I selected the Central zone. Ken and I were happy with the size limit, we rarely took anything undersized, but from then on, we had to take a measuring device with us underwater to make sure we didn't pick up any that could have been a bit undersized. If we were examined by Fisheries and Games inspectors and found to have even one undersized ab on board, they could confiscate the whole catch.

As the year progressed, our income had shrunk considerably because there were too many unlicensed divers depleting the more accessible reefs in Port Phillip Bay. Inspectors were everywhere, and sometimes we were inspected twice a day. They would even turn up at the canneries to make sure no one was buying anything undersized.

To make it more difficult, my son David was born in May, and we then had to rely only on the one income. Ken and his fiancé Julie had plans to marry, and all of this meant that we both had to spend time working sometimes in awful conditions when the visibility underwater was next to nil in order to make ends meet.

In mid-August we received our Master Fisherman's licence and it was endorsed for taking Abalone in the Central Zone only. The $200 cost had to be paid by the 1st of September (1968). From that time on, no more Abalone licences were to be issued.

A lot of divers were incensed that they had to pay $200 and refused. They went looking for work elsewhere.

Even Ken was in two minds about paying the $200 fee. Being a boner, he could easily get a well-paid job at the meat-works. But I convinced him to pay it. I went to the bank that was handling our home loan and borrowed the money from them to pay for the licence.

What pissed off a lot of divers was that the licence had to be renewed each year, and they all mumbled about the reefs being depleted and that in a few years there wouldn't be enough abalone to support the industry anyway.

Out of the more than 400 registered divers, so many refused to pay or renew their licence that the numbers after September dropped to 72 divers in the Central Zone, that being the biggest area, 35 in the Eastern Zone, and approximately 20 in the Western Zone.

This meant that Ken and I had Port Phillip Bay almost all to ourselves, with only 10 divers in the Bay area. The others in the central zone were scattered all along the coast from Wilson's Promontory to Apollo Bay, some 800 kilometres of coastline.

The first $200 licence. Prior to this the abalone diver's licence had only been $4. A bloody big jump which many divers refused to pay.

As an aside: Zara's parents offered to pay for us to take a trip to Germany so she and young David could meet my parents, whom I hadn't seen for 14 years. We were to be away for ten months before returning at the end of September 1969, returning via Canada and the USA. (*This will be covered in a separate memoir that follows my first book Journey of a Lifetime*).

Ken agreed to be a border in our house while we were away as well as to pay me some rent for use of our Riviera. He also took care of my next Abalone Licence due in July but which had to be paid by September, so with all that arranged I felt much better about taking an extended trip overseas.

In the last few days before Zara, David and I were due to fly to Germany, we worked very hard, mostly at Kirk's Point where there were still some productive reefs. That little bit of extra money we earned was sorely needed if we were to be away for a long time.

We left the week before Christmas 1968.

The Central Zone

Part Three

More adventures in The Bay and in Bass Strait

Getting back into it

We got back from Germany by the end of October 1969, and Zara who had never spoken a word of German before the trip was now quite fluent with the language.

The first thing Ken told me was that it had been pretty tough at first diving by himself, but he met another licensed diver from Williamstown, Doug Bear, and they had become good friends. They had joined forces and were working well together.

"One of Doug's friends was the manager of South Pacific Canneries," he said, "and he's been buying our Abs at a good price. A bit better than what we'd been getting before you left." He also told me that he and Julie had paid off a block of land near Sunbury for $2,500 and that they were considering to build a house there.

"On top of that," he added, I also paid the $200 to the Fisheries and Game for your Ab licence, as promised."

I found out that Les Tuckey was now only buying abalone from selected divers, and that he was more focused on scallops.

South Pacific Canneries only bought shucked abalone meat, which meant having to do that again on board after we finished the day's diving. I was anxious to get back into the water but was worried that having not dived for almost a year, I wouldn't be able to keep up with Ken Doug, but I needn't have worried. After a couple of days back in the water, I was doing as well as I had before. With Doug, Ken and myself as a trio, it worked out well. Every day we dived we changed, with two in the water while the third took a turn at shucking what was brought up and keeping an eye on the two below. Most of the Bay meat we delivered to South Pacific Canneries, but sometimes we took it to Russell Crayfish, or when we worked down at Torquay, we sold the greens to Blackney Seafoods in Geelong.

On a two or three day run we put in at Queenscliff and stayed at the Pub, with diving days at Cheviot or Barwon Heads. This first-class ocean blacklip we would sell to Les Tuckey, or sometimes even to Smorgons. Selling to different processors meant we kept our foot in the door and didn't miss out on a pay rise when they paid a better price.

We did very well and I noticed the abalone population had grown significantly with lots of size abalone for two obvious reasons: the lesser amount of legally registered divers working, since many had not paid the increased fee and had dropped out of the industry, and because the Fisheries and Games inspectors patrolled well enough to keep the unlicensed divers and poachers out of the water.

We worked approximately 10 months with Doug, but then one morning in September in 1970, after a couple of bad days of weather with no diving anywhere, we received terrible news. Doug had been killed in a car crash.

He had been travelling along Kororoit Creek Road late in the afternoon on his way home when he crashed into a lamp post and was killed. He was the only person in the car. We never found out how it had happened. It was a big shock to the system because we'd been working really well together… and now he was gone. Ken and I were by ourselves again.

Hans Heidemann, a self-employed carpenter who did some work on our house, and who lived in Altona, offered to become our deckhand. That suited us, because with a deckhand, we could both work underwater safely. And if the weather wasn't good for diving, Hans could work as a carpenter, doing repairs and renovations.

A Fish Story

At the end of September, ken and I visited the Victorian Boat Show at the Exhibition Buildings in Melbourne and were greeted warmly by Howard Roberts and his Partner Tom at the Savage boat section. We knew Tom. He had the Ampol service station in Millers Road, around the corner from our house where we usually bought whatever fuel we needed. He also had an adjacent block where he sold the boats Howard Roberts Marine traded in on new purchases. Howard showed us his latest boat, the new Savage 18.2-foot Ensign, and we were rapt with it. A beautiful looking boat. Tom immediately offered to let us try out a demonstration model that he kept at the lot next to his service station. We instantly agreed to do exactly that.

A couple of days later, during the first week in October I drove our Dodge Ute across to Tom's Ampol service station to pick up the Ensign they were allowing us to try out; to test drive, so to speak. He offered us a good trade in price for our Riviera as a sweetener.

While I was hooking the trailer with the boat onto the Ute, I asked him if he could sell me a couple of hand-lines and some bait. We were going to see if we could catch some fish while we tested the new boat.

He just chuckled as he handed me the fishing lines and the bait. "Who do you think you are, Houdini?"

I must add here that two days earlier ken and I had bought 20 pounds of squid and octopus, on Ken's suggestion that we should try and catch some fish while we were testing the Ensign and not diving. Ken explained about long-line fishing in Queensland, that we should make a couple of long lines baited with about 100 hooks, which we could drop over the side and drag along as we tested the boat. Ken was also an expert at catching mud crabs. It took us a while to bait and prepare the two long lines which we put into two boxes. The boxes went into the boot of Ken's car and he then waited for me at Seaholme, the boat launching place at Altona.

Tom and a couple of people there in the lot laughed at me as I started to drive off towing the Ensign. I headed down Millers Road towards Altona. At the boat ramp at Seaholme, Ken was waiting to give me a hand to launch the Ensign. When I asked about the boxes, he immediately taped his lips with his forefinger. "Shhh… we have to be very careful. What we are going to do is highly illegal."

There were a few people around even though it was in the middle of the week. When the Ensign was in the water, Ken looked around to make sure the coast was clear. He then went and got the two boxes of baited fish lines from the boot of his car and we put them into the boat. He chucked a couple of hessian bags over the boxes in case someone looked inside the boat.

As soon as we took off, we liked the boat and the way it handled. Even though the Bay was flat, with hardly any breeze to ruffle the water, we knew that this boat would handle anything the Bay could produce. This was the boat for us.

We went to the old ammunition pier between Altona and Point Cook, and making sure the coast was clear, he uncovered the boxes. There was no one anywhere near the old pier on the beach or in boats on the water.

"Start driving towards Brighton," he told me.

He started to drop the baited hooks over the side as we moved along. Each hook hung beneath the line weighted with small lead weights to keep it down under the water. The beginning and end of the long line the hooks hung from was marked with cork to keep it near the surface so we could see it. Once the first line was set, we headed towards Point Cook, where we repeated the process, this time heading from Point Cook towards Frankston. After that we had a bit of a rest while Ken smoked a Camel. He loved his Camel cigarettes.

There was hardly anyone on the Bay fishing since it was midweek and most amateur fishermen were at work. After half an hour we went to the first line we'd dropped and easily found it because of the cork floaters, and Ken started pulling it in as I drove the boat slowly forwards. I saw a golden shimmer in the water as I watched Ken pull up a big Snapper on the first hook. The next also yielded a Snapper, then there was a big Rock Ling, a couple of Gummy sharks. He also got a couple of Stingrays and some more Snapper. By the time we got to the last hook the whole floor of the boat was covered with fish.

After another break and another Camel, it was time to bring up the second line which was just as full of fish as the first.

"It's time to head back," ken said. As I started the motor, he called out, "Hang on a minute." He grabbed the bait I'd bought from Tom and threw most of it over the side. He unwound the fishing lines to make it look as if we'd used them. The long lines we'd actually used he put back into the boxes which would go back into the boot of his car once we got back to the boat ramp. "Okay, now we can go."

After winching the Ensign back onto its trailer, we headed back to Tom's. We passed by my place where Ken left his car. He joined me in the Ute and we drove around the corner to Tom's service station and the lot with the boats for sale.

It had been almost four hours from the time I'd picked up the boat earlier, and Tom and his mechanic were talking with a customer when we arrived.

"How'd you like the boat?" Tom called out as we drove in.

"No good Tom," I yelled back.

He quickly finished with the customer and came over to talk to us. We were beside the boat unhooking the trailer.

"What's wrong with it?" He looked worried.

"It's too white. It hurts our eyes." I told him.

"What…?"

"If we could get a different colour, we would buy it," I said.

That made his eyes light up, and then he grinned as he realized we'd been teasing him.

"Did you catch any fish?"

"Just a couple," Ken said.

"They're in the boat," I added. "Have a look."

He stepped on the trailer's mudguard, hauled himself up and looked over the side.

"Shit!" he uttered, his face pale. He straightened up and almost fell backwards of the mudguard. I held him to stop him falling. He took another look in the boat where all the fish were, then slowly stepped back down and walked off towards his office shaking his head.

"I can't believe what I just saw," he told his staff inside and they all came outside to have a look for themselves.

Ken made sure the hand lines I'd bought were visible.

While everyone looked inside the boat at the fish, Tom said, "I might as well throw my fancy fishing rods in the tip for all the good they've been over the last year. These two bloody amateurs with a couple of hand lines and a bit of bait they wanted to pass the time while testing the boat have caught more fish than I've ever done. I can't believe it. A whole boatload in a couple of hours!"

He wandered off shaking his head.

We unloaded the fish and gave the biggest Snapper to Tom.

The rest of the fish we loaded into our Ute and took home to put in the big fridge. Apart from a couple we kept for ourselves to eat, we sold most of it over the next two days. That also included a small Wobbegong shark that Ken filleted after we got back home.

Ken, ready to fillet the shark in the driveway beside the service station.

We never told Tom the truth about how we caught all the fish, and when he retired and moved to his home town Echuca, he would surely have told this story, no doubt with considerable embellishment, to all of his friends there.

The Central Zone

A new boat

Through Tom and Howard's Marine, we had Savage build us a special commercial Ensign with an orange deck and a white hull. It was powered with a 115 HP Evinrude on the back, Peter built and fitted a bow rail and all our dive gear.

Our New Ensign at Peter's place about to be fitted with a bow rail.

All ready to go, with a decent bow rail, and all our equipment on board.

In 1972 we also had to nominate a deckhand and pay for a Master Fisherman's licence for him, which entitled us to take Mussels, Sea-Urchins and Beche-de-Mer. This extra licence cost $30 and was of course separate from my Abalone Licence.

Sometimes we had John Morlock as a deckhand, and other times when Hans wasn't working as a carpenter, he came with us. With a deckhand both of us could get a lot of diving in and we made some very good hauls. John Morlock later went into harvesting Mussels for sale to local restaurants, before eventually moving to Tasmania.

Every time we worked the ocean our daily catch was always between five or six bins of meat while in the Bay it was up to four bins.

Four bins of first class black lip abalone from The Bay.

According to my diary and the sales dockets I still have, Ken and I worked 250 days every year. Most registered divers did the same.

Back on the Mintak

It was the end of September and we had just delivered a load to Melbourne Seafoods when Les Tuckey came out to tell us that the Mintak was ready to do a trial run with a new skipper Greg Huggins, along with several divers. "Are you guys interested in joining us?"

Sensing a new adventure, we immediately agreed.

"What happened to the idea of dredging for scallops?"

"Wasn't a good idea."

That's all he said. Didn't matter, we would be happy to be diving off the Mintak again.

Peter Buckingham, Greg Huggins (Skipper), Noel Middlecoat, John Cadwalader, Fred Glasbrenner, and Rick Harris.

All the divers on board the Mintak had been selling to Les for some time, and they often socialized together. This made it easy for Les to select a great team.

Several days later, we left the wharf and headed for Port Phillip Bay Heads. Once through the Heads, we expected to turn to the East to head towards Wilson's Promontory, but Greg, the skipper, set course for King Island,

"We have to give the Mintak a good run with her new twin motors, and the open waters of Bass Strait are as good as anywhere," he explained.

"We'll go where ever you go," someone said, which was redundant because we had no other option but to go where ever the skipper decided he would go. Greg was a long time cray and shark fisherman from Apollo Bay and he knew all the reefs between there and King Island.

The Mintak performed extremely well, cruising at a leisurely 10 knots, and at daybreak the next morning we anchored close to the shoreline on top of some reefs near Currie, the main town and administrative centre for the island.

The water was crystal clear and on my first dive I could hardly believe the size and abundance of both green and black lip abalone covering the reef. There were fish everywhere, and so many crayfish you couldn't count them. What a fantastic spot.

With four divers in the water, and me with my parachute on my back, I was able to help the others with lifting their full sacks of abalone to the surface. Even though we were in shallow waters it was still hard to get a full sack up to the surface with just swimming and dragging. We still had to shell the Abs on deck and fill plastic bins with the meat.

We worked there for two days, only shifting once. But early the following morning a sou-westerly started to blow and Greg suggested we move to the east of the island, where he knew there were some good reefs to check out. We weren't going to dive for abalone, because we already had a boatload of meat. We spent some time checking the reefs which were really good, and to which we figured we would come back to on another day, before heading for Grassy, the island's only harbour. We were about to anchor near several professional fishing boats when Greg Yelled "Fisheries." He put the Mintak in reverse to turn and as soon as that was done it was full throttle out of the harbour and into the Strait.

As he did this, we noticed a couple of uniformed guys pulling up anchor where they were in amongst several other boats. One of the guys on that boat was watching us through binoculars.

"What the hell is going on?" one of the divers asked Greg. "Why the sudden rush to leave?"

"Anyone can come to King Island to fish," Greg said as he gripped the wheel, "but diving for abalone without a Tasmanian Licence is a definite NO-NO. If they catch us, they'll confiscate the catch, and maybe even the Mintak."

We all knew that we'd been poaching, but had no idea the law in Tassie was so severe.

We headed directly out into the Strait on a course for Port Phillip Heads,

Peter Buckingham, shucking and sorting the abs on deck.

We absolutely loved crayfish...

with the fisheries boat about a half a mile behind us. It was getting dark and Greg deliberately didn't put on our running lights. But somehow the fisheries guys following could still see us. They didn't seem to be getting any closer, but we hadn't lost them either. We could see them because they had their running lights on. It was then one of the guys realized we had a long flame shooting out of one of the engines' exhaust pipes. As soon as one of the guys put a wet hessian bag over the exhaust pipe, we became invisible in the dark. Greg instantly changed course and headed towards Apollo Bay instead of Port Phillip Heads.

"Have we lost them?" we asked Greg.

"They appear to be holding the same course as before."

We watched anxiously for a while, until we could no longer see their running lights.

"Yeah, we've lost them," Greg said. And we all sighed with relief.

We anchored in Apollo Bay and straight away unloaded the bins of abalone into the back of Greg's double axle trailer and by 2 am the load was on its way to Melbourne Seafoods and was sold to them by 6am.

We stayed in Apollo Bay for a few days and explored the coast back towards Port Phillip Heads, during which time we delivered quite a few bins of meat. Ken and I made close to $500 each over this short time. We were known as Tuckey's Renegades for a long time after that little adventure.

On examination, there was not much wrong with the Mintak or its motors, but the faulty exhaust pipe was replaced with a new one and she headed for Wilson's Promontory with the same dive crew, minus Ken and me, because we'd decided that we would be happy to be working from our new Ensign exploring most of the central region, which we were licensed to dive in.

Ken getting the boat ready for work,   In the water with Hans, our deckhand.

Ken and Julie got married and they built a house in Frazer Avenue Altona, and had two lovely children, Ben and Marnie.

Mervin, Ken's best man, Ken and Fred, ready for Ken's and Julie's wedding.

Julie and Ken

Around this time, someone came up with the idea of making abalone bags out of fishnet, held together by a stainless-steel ring with an abalone measure welded on top of the ring, also with a heavy plastic bag as a parachute to lift the full bag off the bottom so it didn't have to be dragged along. It also made it so easy to float a full bag up to the surface and the waiting boat that there was no need any more for the parachute I strapped to my back.

With the parachute inflated, it was easy to take large bags of abalone up the surface from any depths.

Ken and I worked as a great team together for eight years, diving for Mussels and Sea Urchins, and there were lots of adventures during that time.

Several times, we towed our Ensign to Port Campbell, but it was a nightmare even though we found many good patches of reef to work. Launching

The pier at Port Campbell where boats are launched and retrieved by using a crane. There were no boats being launched on the day this photo was taken because the sea was too rough.

Locals didn't seem bothered by the boat launching method. Below: a boat about to be launched. Left: Swung out over the edge and on its way down.

our boat by crane into the sea was always a huge hassle especially when coming back with a boatload Abalone that had to be lifted out with the crane on the dock. We had to stay in motels which were costly because the whole area is geared up for tourists, and then having to transport the bins of Abalone all the way to Geelong, or sometimes even back to Melbourne, became too costly. After a couple of runs we gave it a miss.

Going separate ways

Around June 1975, when the price of ocean Abalone was 28cents a pound, Ken, after lots of pondering, decided he would go his own way. We traded our Ensign in for two Savage Escorts and Ken moved to Apollo Bay to live and work. He built a beautiful house there. I stayed and worked Port Phillip Bay by myself.

A new beginning

It was a very strange feeling to be diving by myself, but after a few days I began to get used to it. I was now my own boss and could do whatever I thought necessary without having to consult Ken.

But by myself it was unwise to go out in a boat, and finding a good spot, switch on the compressor and start diving alone, underwater with no one in the boat above.

I asked my younger brother-in-law Paul if he wanted to come out with me as a deckhand. He was on a break from his university studies and readily agreed. After he had to go back to Uni, I hired John Morlock as a deckhand. John was an expert on mussels, and wanted to start his own mussel farm, so he only worked with me a short time before Paul Will became my third deckhand. And then there was Paul Buttigieg, a Maltese fisherman who loved the ocean, who was a deckhand for me for the longest time.

Paul Litchen as a deckhand, holding a black lip from Point Cook.

Getting ion and out of the water at Altona was sometimes a sticky business if the tide was out.

Paul Buttigieg my long-time deckhand, with the Miranda at Altona.

Paul hauling up a large load from the reefs at Point Cook.

I worked the Savage Escort for several years, selling most of the time to Pacific Canneries and Safcol, until I traded the Escort in on a Shark Cat. By then I'd also purchased a Volkswagen Camper-Van and that combination gave me a lot of leeway. I no longer had to pay for expensive motel accommodation while away.

I slept in the Camper Van.

The Central Zone

My campervan parked in front of the Shark Cat, at Queenscliff.

When the forecast for the weather was good, I would launch the Cat at Queenscliff, and could motor as far along the coast as Cape Schanck, or the other way towards Anglesea and Aireys Inlet. If I dived in that area for a couple days or more, I could leave my catch at the Fishermen's Co-op, and then once I had accumulated enough, I only had to make one trip to the cannery with a good load rather than a few trips with smaller loads.

Being by myself, sometimes I would relax by watching fish in their natural habitat. Using an upturned abalone as bait. Within moments a leather-jacket would appear and start eating the ab. It would very soon be joined by others and a small feeding frenzy would occur.

Leather-jackets feasting on an injured abalone.

A serious threat appears

From 1977, conditions on my licence changed and I was only allowed to take Abalone and Mussels. It really didn't bother me that much because we had begun to encounter a real threat to the industry, a predatory starfish called ***Coscinasterias Calamaria.*** This was a huge, eleven-armed starfish that preyed on shellfish of all kinds.

The first time I noticed this starfish was under the Williamstown Lighthouse. I also saw it under different piers around the Bay, and sometimes, I'd seen them grazing on a few reefs where we collected good abalone. I never took much notice of them in the early days of diving because they were not so prevalent. They were just there, like other smaller starfish and other marine creatures.

Coscinasterias Calamaria devouring baby mussels on pylons under a pier

I had no idea where they came from, but suddenly they were everywhere; millions of them, and they ate anything their tentacles could get hold of. Sedentary shellfish like mussels, or clams and ascidians were easy prey, because they couldn't move from their fixed position on pier piles or on rocks in a reef. Even Abalone or Sea Urchins, which could move or crawl away from danger couldn't escape this monster. The starfish could move faster, and would get on top of an Abalone whether it was moving or stuck on a rock, and keep pulling until the animal's muscle would weaken slightly. The starfish would then flip it over and extruding its stomach, would start digesting the animal it had in its grip.

Why had their numbers exploded to such an extent so quickly? There were probably a number of explanations, but the one that seems most probable to me is because this monster of a starfish could reproduce in two ways, sexually (with two mating) and asexually, with one, if broken, or torn in half, each part able to regrow the damaged area, thus becoming two new individuals. Coscinasterias Calamari was one of a few creatures that could completely regrow any part that was missing.

The explosive number of these creatures is quite possibly linked to the discovery of scallops in Port Phillip Bay. In the early sixties, the scallop beds were so vast that a new industry of dredging for scallops began. Suddenly there were scallop boats everywhere. Most of them had big hydraulic dredges on the transom with a sorting platform in front. The dredges were dragged along the bottom with steel cables to catch the scallops which were fast moving and could jump several times their height off the bottom by snapping their shells shut and expelling water. That didn't help them to escape the dredge which scooped up everything. The dredge scooped up everything in its way, seaweed, rocks, lots of fish, as well as Coscinasterias Calamari starfish.

After the dredge's contents were sorted on board the boat, the scallops were put into hessian bags stacked on the deck, bay oysters and some fish were put in buckets and kept separate, while whatever was left was simply thrown back overboard. In amongst the stuff thrown overboard were sometimes quite a few of the predatory starfish. Many of those were damaged or had arms torn off. The workers on the boat didn't know that each bit of a damaged starfish could regrow into a completely new one, and instead of throwing back half a dozen damaged starfish, they were throwing back many more times that number.

Apart from this, thousands of amateur fishermen who fished daily in the Bay, and who had no idea of what that starfish was capable of, whenever they brought one to the surface that might have been attacking their bait, they would curse, chop it into pieces and throw it back. They thought chopping it into pieces killed it. But no, it didn't. Each piece was capable of growing back, regenerating the rest of what was missing to become a new (cloned) starfish.

It was truly astonishing. A lizard can grow back a tail that it loses, or even a leg perhaps. Cut off an octopus tentacle and the octopus will regrow a replacement, although the severed tentacle won't or can't grow into a new octopus. But with Coscinasterias Calamaria, if you chop off an arm or two, the creature will regrow new arms to replace the missing ones. But it also has the ability for each arm, (cut or chopped or broken off) to regenerate a whole new creature, so instead of having one starfish with parts missing you have however many parts there are missing each becoming a new starfish as well as the original one repairing itself.

The scallop boats moved on when the Bay was so over-fished there was hardly enough scallops left for scallop fishermen to make a living. But for quite a few years these boats and their hideous dredges completely tore up and ravaged the bottom of the Bay. When they left, millions of starfish crawled over everything under the surface eating whatever they could without any natural enemies to control them.

Nothing was safe from these starfish. Creatures like these beautiful ascidians and mussels which grow and live fixed to rocks and pylons were particularly vulnerable to the voracious appetite of Coscinasterias Calamaria.

The Central Zone

Advancing from the murky water a monster approaches mussels and ascidians on a pylon beneath a pier.

The sharp spines of a sea urchin do not put off the starfish.

I grabbed one off a bed of mussels and this is what I found under the starfish, two partly eaten mussels.

I called several local newspapers because they were always looking for material that was local for their weekly papers, and they sent reporters to interview me after which they wrote stories about the starfish and the damage they were causing to the underwater environment. My brother in law, John, who sometimes accompanied me on various dives to photograph and film me in action contacted channel 9 TV station and they sent a reporter to do a special story. The reporter Stewart Scocroft and a team of photographers and a sound recordist came with us in two boats out to one of my favourite reefs off Point Cook to see for themselves the menace these starfish were to the Bay. John shot the underwater sequences while the news team did the above water shots. The story appeared the same night on television.

Not to be outdone, Channel 7 approached us and they also did a story on the starfish menace. A week later the ABC also did a story using the film john had shot for the fist TV news broadcast. He shot a lot of film over a couple of weeks apart from what was shot specifically for channel 9 on the day they came out with us. We also had the Age newspaper and the Herald Sun do stories on the starfish as well. There was a lot of talk about what could be done, but in reality, not much actually could be done to stop the starfish. It was already too late. They didn't appear to have any natural predators and once they had decimated the Bay, they would either die out (of starvation) or would move out of the Bay into the ocean. In time the Bay would recover.

Bringing up a handful of starfish for the TV crew to see. Being interviewed by Stewart Scocroft on board my boat. I am explaining to him how the starfish eats an abalone. Once the starfish has weakened the abalone's grip on the rock it turns it over, then extrudes its stomach to begin dissolving and absorbing the flesh of the abalone.

The Central Zone

Starfish are taking over in bay

By Ron Coleman

Starfish are eating the life out of Port Phillip Bay and seriously threatening the fishing industry.

These claims were made last week by a man who spends much of his life under water.

He is Fred Glasbrenner, an abalone diver of May Street, Altona North.

"The starfish are taking over our natural reefs and devouring everything in their path ... jellyfish, crabs, abalone, mussels, all kinds of shellfish, even spiny sea urchins and seaweed," he said.

Fred has been diving professionally in the bay for 11 years and says he's never seen anything like it.

"The situation has got so bad in the last couple of years that if they keep going all that will be left is bare reef."

The starfish Fred refers to are the 'coscinasteni as calamaria' species.

They each have 11 tentacles and a stomach which drops out from their body allowing them to choke the life out of shellfish and vegetation.

On an average dive, Fred kills about 100 starfish and...

Abalone fishing depends on weather conditions.

"Sometimes we can't work for three weeks."

Fred also seeks co-operation from other abalone divers in killing starfish in the bay and bringing them out of the water.

"If each boat brought out a bagful a day, we could hold them back," he said.

After talking to Fred, I contacted Conrad Beinssen, officer-in-charge of marine fisheries research at the Fisheries and Wildlife Department.

He agreed there had been a "dramatic increase" of starfish in certain spots.

REMOVAL

Mr. Beinssen said research carried out by fisheries people in Qu...

One of many newspaper articles about the starfish menace in Port Phillip Bay. Sometimes I would leave my bag in one spot while collecting more abalone only to discover on returning that starfish were crawling over it to get at the abalone inside.

Friedrich Glasbrenner

John, filming Coscinasterias Calamaria.

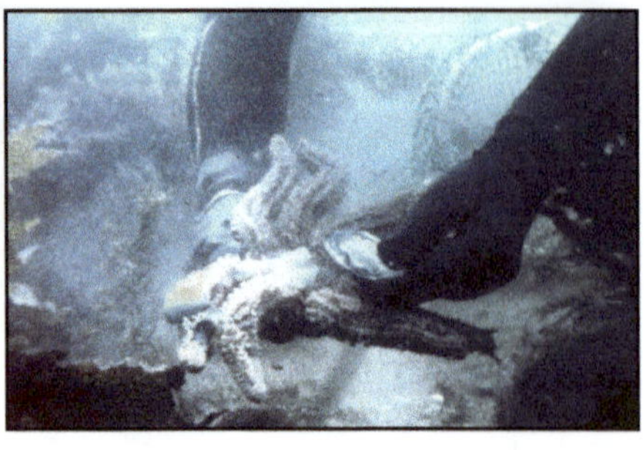

Scenes from the TV news film of a starfish attacking an abalone, of Fred picking up a starfish to show it already eating an abalone.

The Central Zone

Above:
They might look colorful, but these starfish swarming over a reef are a deadly menace to anything else that lives there.

Partly eaten abalone, and recently emptied shells collected within a few minutes from one small part of the reef. The arms of one of the culprits are seen at the edge of the photo.

Fred with the Channel 9 news team finishing their shoot at the Seaholme boat ramp.

A collection of shells of various sizes, all of which he found on the bottom.
They had been stripped clean by Coscinasterias Calamaria, and it didn't matter what size they were, they were all food for the voracious starfish.

I tried as much as possible to tell people about this underwater menace, through interviews with newspapers and magazines, and tried to explain the only way to get rid of them was to collect them and take them out of the water to let them dry up and wither in the sun. Never chop them up and throw the bits back in, because each bit will become a new starfish.

It became impossible for me to work the Bay and most of the time from then on, I had to work out in the ocean, which was much harder. But still, I managed to earn enough to pay the bills and to pay off our mortgage.

More regulations

In 1978, being commercial fishermen, we had to do a course at the Marine Board of Victoria. We had to choose between a Coxswain Ticket to skipper a boat up to 30 feet in length, or a Master V Class Ticket for a boat up to 60 feet. Ken and I went for the Master V Class which meant we had to undertake two more days of examinations.

Today still, deckhands must have Coxswain Tickets, because abalone boats are mostly up to 23 feet in length.

On the 14th of February, Valentine's Day, my daughter Dione was born.
Later that year we sold our house in North Altona and moved to a 150-year-old heritage protected Victorian house in Cecil Street Williamstown. A driving school, the Williamstown Motor School, a business run by the previous owners of the house in Cecil Street was also transferred to us, and Zara looked after this business while I concentrated on abalone diving and the establishment of AAE, Australian Abalone Exports. Life became busier than ever...

Our house in North Altona, as it looked when we sold it in 1978.

The Central Zone

Part Four

A new venture

Friedrich Glasbrenner

Kevin Carboon and Rob Baran in Rob's boat at Cape Schanck.

The Birth of AAE: Australian Abalone Exports

Kevin Carboon.

When the weather was good, I pulled the boat down to Apollo Bay, because the beach price was much better. Barry Parton accompanied me as a deckhand on these occasions.

"I still remember, when Friends and neighbours asked how long it took us to get to Apollo Bay? We told them, six stubbies."

It was a few days before Xmas 79, and we were having a drink at our house in Williamstown with a few Divers and Deckhands, when Kevin Carboon suggested, that one or two of us should start buying Abs and re-selling them ourselves.

We hadn't thought of that before, and it took a while for the idea to sink in. We discussed it for some time and finally, Rob Baran and I decided to give it a go.

We bought an International Truck and with the help of John Thynne and Barry Parton we fitted it out as a shucking shed on wheels.

By mid 1980 we registered **AAE: *Australian Abalone Exports*.**

It had started out well, because several of our divers sold to us and all Barry and John had to do was pick the abalone up from the boat ramps at St Kilda or Williamstown.

They shucked the Abs late afternoon and delivered them to SPC the next morning. Word slowly spread that Rob and I were buying Abs, because one day I got a call from a licensed Abalone Diver in Adelaide, who offered us small Greenlip meat, which he'd had difficulty selling in SA.

He brought us a sample, which we took to Russell Crayfish PL, where we were offered 60 cents a pound. We told the Diver we could pay him 50 cents a pound if he would pay the freight to the Airport.

Checking the samples from South Australia... Small greenlip abalone.

He agreed and sent the first 10 sealed buckets, holding up to 30 pounds each by Ansett Freight, where either Barry or John picked them up and delivered them straight to Russell Crayfish.

It worked out really well for nearly two years, especially since we averaged close to 2000 pounds every week.

Rob left the running of AAE entirely to me and because of domestic problems he moved to Phillip Island and eventually sold his catch to the local processor.

With him not on the scene, Theo, my very close friend in Germany suggested that I should buy him out.

"Offer him $10,000 for his share. I'll send you the money."

I was a bit hesitant, but Theo insisted. "Do it, and see what he says."

Rob of course was delighted to be offered so much money.

He immediately accepted. We sorted out the paper work with Solicitors and Accountants and within less than a month, I was the sole Director of AAE (Australian Abalone Exports).

Nothing of course runs smoothly.

The DPI (Department of Primary Industry) wouldn't register our truck as an export premises, and the Fisheries and Game weren't too happy with us buying and shucking in the truck. We were told numerous times to lease

Friedrich Glasbrenner

Colin Turner enjoying a beer at my place in Williamstown.

licensed premises or they would shut us down.

It was around that time when **SPC**: ***Shepparton Preservative Canneries*** took part in the Abalone Industry and bought out (SPC): ***South Pacific Canneries.***

Collin Turner became the Manager of their Collingwood Factory.

I will always remember Collin for the great help he gave me in Business, as well as being a long time Friend.

A true gentleman indeed.

After a long discussion with Collin Turner, we had meetings with the Board of Directors from SPC at the factory in Islington Street Collingwood and it was decided, that I would be able to lease their premises after working hours at $80 per week. This was Actually one of the best moves I ever made!

Unfortunately, my friend John Thynne moved to New Zealand with his family to be with his son, leaving Barry to handle the truck and pick up the Abs by himself.

Nick Apostopolou, who worked for SPC, offered with his wife to shuck the Abs in the evening, that meant Barry only had to pick up the empty shells early next morning and take them to the local tip. This helped me a lot and I could concentrate on my own diving.

I dare say that I worked my butt off, spending every conceivable day under water, mainly in Port Phillip Bay, in good weather or bad. I still dived my 250 days per year, as I had done with Ken and I could sell as much as I could catch.

In all those years we had size limits, but we could catch as much as we wanted. 100 mm in Port Phillip, 105 mm east of Port Phillip Heads and 115 mm west.

I felt great as a director, and when the money kept coming my way pretty fast, I kept wandering: What if I had my own factory? What if I canned the Abs myself? I could become a great Exporter.

After discussions with Collin, my family and some of my diving friends,

Angus Scott-Walker relaxing under a palm tree.

I got to know Angus Scott-Walker, a real estate Agent in Footscray, who suggested I should buy a block of land at the Industrial Area in Laverton North, which was not far from Williamstown.

"You can build your own export factory," he said on a number of occasions.

Having had a considerable amount of money saved, I decided to do it. At the end of 1980 I put a deposit on a reasonably sized site at 15 Plummer Road Laverton North, and Angus helped with the paperwork and documents which concluded with me receiving the title for the land in 1981.

I must add here that Angus became a very close friend and is still one to this day.

Friedrich Glasbrenner

Plans Approved

Plans for the proposed abalone export factory were approved and work could get started, except there was one small problem, Money! I simply didn't have anywhere near enough. I heard about the *Victorian Economic Development Corporation* (VEDC) and got in touch with them. They approved a $150.000.00 loan at 6 per cent interest. And so we got started.

There was a lot of rubbish on the site and this all had to be cleared, old building materials, bits of wood, broken bricks, iron bars, stuff builders on neighbouring sites dumped instead of taking it away to the tip. We had to clear all that before we could start anything else.

As the summer approached and the ground dried out we started with the framework. I was happy to see that go up and couldn't keep away from the site as the building was being constructed.

Here I am after the floor had been laid and the first cool room was put in place. It was starting to take shape. I could hardly believe it!

The Central Zone

Victorian Abalone Divers Association

I had been a Member of the *Victorian Abalone Divers Association* (VADA) since its conception and seldom missed a meeting. Later when Victoria was split in three Zones (East, Central and Western Zones) I stayed in the Central Zone, which was the biggest.

It stretched from Hopkins River in the West to Lakes Entrance in the East and had about 72 licensed divers and they lived all over the place. Some of the divers lived up to 800 Km from each other. Sometimes we caught up out at Sea, but most of the time, every couple of months we would get together at a VADA meeting, after which we usually we partied on at the Hotel Australia, and often got home drunk. These were meetings every diver looked forward to, because apart from the socializing we also exchanged diving information, and found out the latests news that could affect us as divers.

One of the contentious issues always discussed was the ever increasing cost of our Abalone Diving Licence. After it had stayed only a few dollars for years it suddenly jumped to $200, at which point a number of divers dropped out, refusing to pay that amount. It remained at $200 for a number of years, but then it started increasing. It went from $200 to $250 with an extra $40 for the deckhand, then it went to $300 with $50 for the deckhand and a year after that it went to $600 with $50 for the deckhand. This huge jump pissed off a lot of divers, but no one really considered giving up their licence at that stage.

We moaned and grumbled about it, but what none of us could have imagined, was how much our licences would increase over the next few years... It very soon became thousands of dollars for an annual licence fee. And with set quota for each zone a licenced diver could bring in a very good income, but without transferability of the licence, you couldn't sell it, and no new divers were allowed to enter the game.

Another threat...

In the very early 1980s we didn't only worry about Starfish; another the big problem was illegal diving.

It took a huge toll on abalone stocks as well as mussels and cockles, mainly in Port Phillip Bay where access to the water was easy. All you had to do was wade out from the beach or the rocks along the foreshore and you could pick off the rocks and the reefs in shallow water as many shellfish as you could. Needless to say, this was not something older Australians did, but was mainly something recent immigrants did. They did this in their home countries so they didn't consider it unusual to do it here. Because of this, the foreshores around the Bay were stripped bare of anything edible, seemingly in no time at all. It probably took a couple of years, which is a really short time when you consider it.

By stripping the shellfish from the reefs easily waded to from the shore, it also affected the fish life. There was hardly anything left close inshore after a couple of years. Some of these people then started swimming out into deeper water and diving down to strip off the shellfish.

Fisheries and Game Inspectors very quickly started to work the foreshores around the Bay and anyone caught fishing illegally or taking abalone and other shellfish were hit with hefty fines. It was not illegal to walk or swim out and to take a few shellfish for your own use, but to take any quantity, was illegal.

Inspectors from the Department of Fisheries and Game checking an illegal catch on the foreshore of the Williamstown Back Beach.

The Central Zone

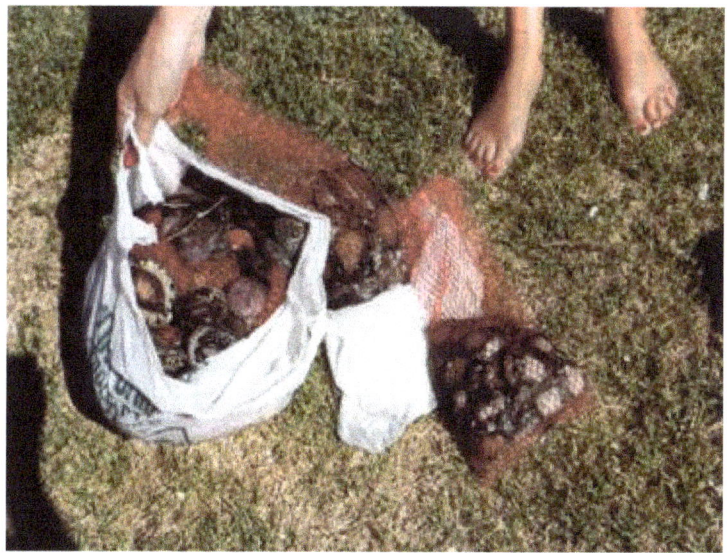

Another illegal catch...

A new boat and a mooring

At that time, there were only a few divers left around Port Phillip Bay. Most of the others moved along the coast and I was almost derogatorily called a Bay Diver. There were a handful of us locals. Fortunately. I knew where there were lots of reefs in deeper water and after spending long hours down below, I still came back with reasonably good catches.

Barry, still picked up from the divers who worked the Bay, but some of the ocean divers delivered straight to SPC, where Victor and his wife took over for me.

By the middle of 1981, I met up with Keith Penfold from *Penfolds Marine* in Douglas Parade Williamstown, who suggested I should get a bigger boat, to be more flexible.

Keith was building Aluminium boats for Savages and he suggested, that he could built a 21 foot "*Swordfish*" for me. I gave it some thought and told him, if he would give me a mooring in his Marina, I would hand him a deposit within a week.

Having had Savage boats for a long time, I knew Keith very well and I knew he would look after me. We shook hands and within 3 month I had a new boat. I had sold our International, because Barry was taking his family back to England, so I bought a near new Isutsu 3-ton double cabin tip truck.

Friedrich Glasbrenner

Contemplating my new **Swordfish** moored at Williamstown.

Taking delivery of my new Swordfish... Parked out front of my house in Cecil Street Williamstown, my wife Zara and her mother had to come out to have a look at it.

A lot of pressure was taken off my back so to speak with the help of some Bay divers, like Ted Aitchison, Noel Middlecoat, Bill Nissan, Ross Brame, (we spent lots of time with Ross and Karin, his deckhand and Partner, on his luxurious dive boat *Vamoose*), Chris Beale, Harry Bishop, Garry Braid, who delivered their catches straight to SPC.

Getting a new Swordfish with a *cuddy* cabin and a mooring, plus a new crane, along with the latest diving equipment made my diving a lot easier.

All I had to do after a small breakfast in the morning, put on my wetsuit and boots, park the truck at Penfolds and jump on the boat to go diving. The boat had a small platform with a folding ladder on the back for easy access.

Sitting on the transom putting on gloves before finally entering the water. You can just see the parachute that supports the collection bag in the water on the left side.

Note the weights. Because my wetsuit was a double layer from the wait up. It consisted of an overall type wetsuit underneath from my feet up to my shoulders, on top of which I put the top half with a hood. Since each part of the wetsuit was 10 millimetres thick, making it 20 millimetres thick from the neck to the waist, I needed additional weights to give me a neutral buoyancy.

If I put all the weights on a single belt, the pressure on my lower back was too much. I had to spread the extra weights above and below the weight belt to keep my body level underwater. I also wore a small weight around each ankle to stop my legs from floating up higher than my back.

Any length of time spent underwater in Port Phillip Bay would suck the body heat out of you. It took a long time before I get a wetsuit like this which could keep me relatively warm for several hours in those freezing waters of the Bay.

Anchored on a reef not far off Williamstown.

Diving and working from this beautiful boat was much easier than from any other I had previously owned. Hauling up a good catch with the crane; rather than trying to drag on board by hand a full bag, was the only way to do it. Once above the water without the parachute to give a neutral buoyancy, a full bag of abalone weighed far too much to comfortably lift on board by hand. Of course we had to do it by hand in the early days before someone invented net bags and parachutes.

Left: getting ready to come back on board after a good day's work. Above: My brother in law, John, who took many of the photos in this book, examining part of that day's catch.

The Francis

I had only worked out of my new boat a couple of times, when Billy Nissen rang me and wanted to know if I was interested to dive from Ted Turner's *Francis* which was a 80 foot Scallop and fishing boat.

"I would be delighted," I told him.

"That's great. Do you know anyone who has a small tinny? Fitted out for diving..."

"As a matter of fact, Chris Beale has one."

"Do you think he might be interested in joining us?"

"Yeah, I reckon."

I immediately rung Chris and he was full on keen. He was always looking for a new adventure and this was right up his alley.

The Francis was moored in Port Welshpool and had just finished unloading fish, when Chris, Wally, Chris's deckhand, and me, towing the tinny behind my truck arrived. Bill and Ron, his long time deckhand, arrived a couple of hours later.

Being a big steel boat, the Francis had huge circulating tanks on a big fore deck, plus a large Kitchen and dining room and it could sleep a dozen people comfortable.

It was decided that we would leave as soon as we got organized. By late afternoon, we headed west towards The Prom and anchored at Refuge Cove, where Ted and his all-rounder treated us to a great dinner. It was decided that our catch should be split between the Francis, Bill, Chris and I, plus all the Abs would go to AAE.

The Central Zone

Early next morning we headed towards the Lighthouse and some of the Islands and by 9 o'clock we were already in the water. Chris and I worked well together and kept Wally busy.

Ron and Bill.

Wally and Chris.

Almost before we knew it, we'd filled half the bins on the deck of the Francis. A couple of hours later we had a full load to take back to Port Welshpool, where they would be loaded onto my truck to take them back for processing.

Friedrich Glasbrenner

The Central Zone

Sorting and unloading the bags as they come up from the divers.

Below: a full day's catch partially sorted before we left to return to Port Welshpool.

Bill, with a gorgeous crayfish he caught for us to have for dinner.
Chris beside Seal Rocks. Right: coming back with a good haul.

Preparing to transfer the catch from the Francis to my truck at Port Welshpool.

We did three runs on the Francis and finished up with just over 12 tonnes of live abalone.

Transferability... at last!

The day of the licence transferability finally arrived and the new regulations became Law. This was sometime in 1984.

That meant that any new diver who would like to join the Abalone Industry, had to buy two licences to obtain one. Not only did the new diver have to buy two licences he also had to pay a transfer fee for each licence to be transferred ($230) he also had to pay a transfer fee for the original diver's annual quota to be transferred ($230). He couldn't get two diver's quotas though; he could only have one.

This was the government's way of controlling the amount of abalone taken in any one year. They had successfully lessened the total number of divers working, and now they wanted to also lessen the annual take in order to maintain the wild stocks. Australia is the only place left in the world where a sustainable wild abalone fishery continues to exist.

Almost immediately a single licence had the value of $80,000 each, making a new licence after transferring from two divers became a cool $160,000.

I think Alan Buck was one of the first deckhands who worked for Clarke Espie to purchase two licences, Bill Middlecoat's and Roy Hebert's, plus Alan supported AAE until the end!

After the first four licenses were sold, a couple of months later the next two went for $120,000.00 each and a short time after that, $150.000.00 each. Very quickly the price of buying a licence escalated to a million plus dollars for one, and when you consider you had to buy two, it became an enormous cost. Nevertheless, there were plenty of people willing to invest in buying two licences, if they could find anyone willing to sell them.

Because our Abalone Licence was now recognized by the Banks as an asset, new divers found it relatively easy to borrow sufficient funds to purchase the two required licenses. That meant that lots of bargaining took place.

Once a licence became transferable it took a lot of financial problems away from several divers, especially those who found it hard to continue diving because of age or health reasons.

Naturally this made it very exciting for some of my diving mates and for me, because all of a sudden, we were all worth a lot of money. I didn't mind that a few of the fellows sold out, but I am happy I didn't; I loved diving too much.

Exciting times

Needless to say, I got very busy with diving on every conceivable day, plus giving a hand to the builders erecting the frame of the factory and looking after SPC.

Some years earlier I had met up with David Ogg from South Australia, who worked at Rheems as a special designer in Melbourne. David used to help me on his days off and after my dives on the Francis he quit his job and became my full time deckhand in the Bay and a good friend.

"Oggie" was also a diver and had a dive boat in Adelaide.

He invited me on a long weekend several years earlier to visit his family and tow his boat, which was in his mother's garage to Robe and dive for Abalone and some Cray's. We got back to his mother's place a couple of days later and David sold the Abs to some Chinese Restaurants, with whom he dealt before.

David was a great help and so were the other divers and friends who stood by us. We all worked hard and the money kept rolling in. I was able to pay the workers and get rid of some Mortgages and that was a hell of a relief.

While all this was happening, I was also having the processing plant built on the land at Laverton North.

Keeping an eye on the builders, looking after our divers as well as diving myself, kept me very busy, but I didn't mind it at all. It was an exciting time for me.

One day I had a surprise visit from Paul Bozinas, who had been working with several divers and was a great diver himself. He knew where there were a lot of Abalone reefs. He made me an offer; I couldn't refuse. Living near Narre Warren where he owned a small farm, he suggested I could use his 23-foot Formula with himself as a deckhand, when the Ocean was flat. (Paul had helped me previously, diving on my Miranda).

All I had to do, was to tow my small trailer with empty bins behind my VW camper and meet him at 9 am at the Hastings or Stony point boat ramps. From there we would go out and dive near Phillip Island, Flinders or Cape Schanck.

It sounded great and I happily took the offer. Paul got paid 2 Dollars a Kg in the shell and I could hardly wait for my first dive. It turned out to be a great move, firstly I got on very well with Paul and secondly, he always had a bottle of Port on board to warm me up on the way back to the ramp, plus he knew a lot of Abalone reefs and became a great Friend.

There was a big difference at the time, between Bay $1.50 beach price per Kg and $ 3.50 for Ocean.

Fred with Paul Bozinas with one of his dive boats on his farm at Narre Warren.

Diving at Cape Schanck

On one particular day, my brother in law John came along with us on a dive at Cape Schanck, so he could record the day's dive 'for posterity'.

The Central Zone

Early in the morning it was overcast as we launched the boat, but the sea was calm and it looked like we would have good diving.

Very soon we were heading out on our way to Cape Schanck.

Paul was incredibly strong, and could easily lift a stack of 10 bins up into the boat.

Fred, relaxed, standing at the stern leaning back on the twin motors as we head out of the harbour. Optimistically we had stacks of empty bins which I was hoping to fill with first class abalone. John's camera bag can be seen in one of the bins.

Cape Schanck and its bommies, a perfect spot to dive for abalone, (and crayfish).

Paul waits while I finish strapping on my lead weights. He had already unwound the hose and had dropped my net bag with its parachute over the side. It would be there just underneath the boat ready for me to grab once I was in the water.

Paul dropped anchor as close as we could safely get to several bommies and I got ready to start diving. Even though it was still overcast, it was a lot brighter. The sea was calm — well, as calm as you would expect out there in the ocean at Cape Schanck. There was still a strong surge as waves rolled in and smashed on the bommies as well as the dragging effect of the water retreating before the next surge, but nothing out of the ordinary.

Stepping down the ladder and into the water.

It was fantastic under the water. There was long strands of sea grass and kelp varieties waving and undulating with the movement of the waves above. The reefs were full of good sized abalone but they were hidden beneath the extensive weed cover. I hardly noticed, but there were times, John said, that he could hardly see me, just my flippers sticking out from under the sea

weed, or the top of the parachute that enabled me to drag along the net bag in which I placed the abalone.

Conditions were perfect and I worked fast and in no time had the first bag filled. As I moved along the bottom Paul up on deck fed out the air hose as I worked my way along the reef.

Once the net bag was full, I inflated the parachute and allowed it to float up to the surface.

The Central Zone

Paul, feeding out the air hose as I swim away from the boat.

Inflating the parachute to carry the bag up to the surface, where Paul is waiting to haul it in.

I follow the bag up and push it towards the boat. Also I hooked the cable from the crane onto the bag so Paul could winch it up onto the boat.

Coming up to help Paul get the first bag on board.

The Central Zone

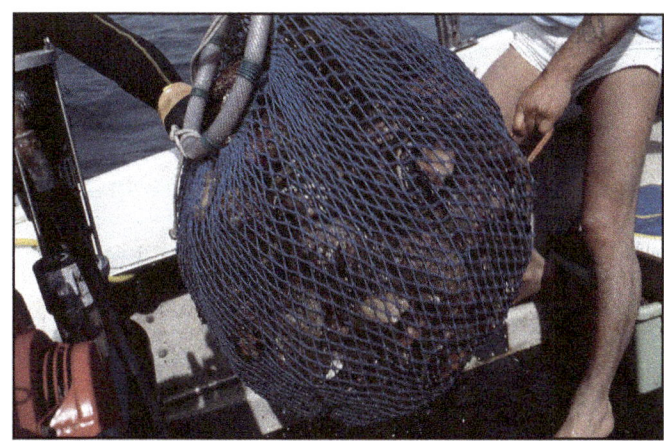

Once the first load was on board, and Paul had started sorting it I went back down again with another bag .

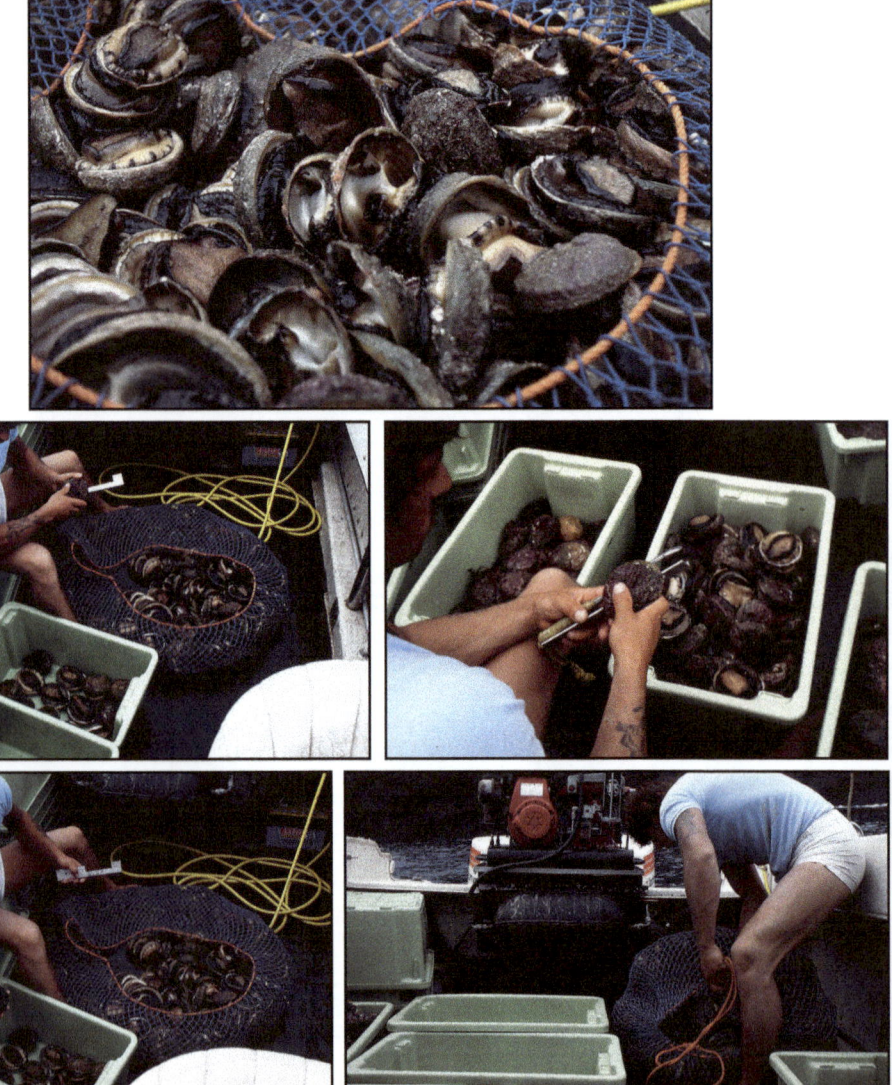

Even though I measured each abalone as I took it off the reef, Paul's job was to check that each one coming out of the bag was not undersize, that they were all legal sized. He usually sorted them into bins based on their size. Sometimes he would sort them straight out of the net bag, but usually, since

The Central Zone

Sometimes I would come across a crayfish hiding underneath a ledge as I prized off abalone, so I would grab it and stuff it in the bag with the abalone already collected.

It was a nice surprise for Paul, who, like the rest of us, loved a good crayfish.

Here he carefully extracts a crayfish from the bag before sorting the abalone into bins.

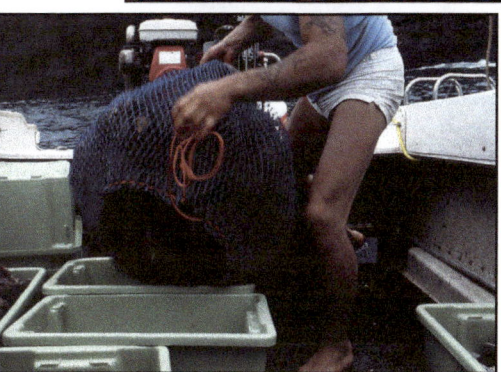 

I needed the bag for the next lot, he would lift the whole bag and dump its contents into a bin or two before sorting them. Those bags when full, were very heavy, and it always amazed me how strong Paul was, to be able to lift one up and upend it dumping its contents.

With all the bins full, I went down just to collect a nice crayfish for dinner that night.

The hardest part of a day's diving was getting out of the wetsuit afterwards.

Paul driving the boat back to Hastings where my trailer and van waited beside the boat ramp.

Starting to transfer the full bins from the boat to my trailer.

By the time we'd offloaded the bins into the trailer I was exhausted, but I still had to drive back to Melbourne, to Collingwood where Victor and Jenny were waiting to shuck my catch, weighing and salting the meat and getting it ready for canning next morning.

I paid my divers always the current beach price, but I (AAE) got paid for the meat.

I worked a long time with Paul and every run we did was mostly four or sometimes five days in a row. Of course we picked good weather which always helped. We didn't always use the same boat because Paul had several different boats which he could use, depending on where we intended to go.

Full bins of abalone stacked in my trailer ready to take back to Melbourne.

Paul's other boat which we used while working from Wilson's Promontory.

Friedrich Glasbrenner

Feeling Happy...

All I can say is that I felt happier as time went on.

Maybe it was that the beach price was creeping up, plus our reefs were becoming healthier again, now that the Starfish population had declined, as well as a lot less illegal diving and poaching, which meant small or undersized abalone were not being taken. I also noticed that weed started to grow again and young Abalone seemed to magically appear on all the once depleted reefs.

Abalone licences had became genuine assets with a lot of bargaining power, and my processing plant at Laverton North was beginning to take shape. The future for me certainly looked promising.

Being on my own, I often wondered whether I had done the right thing in starting to build a factory.

I had no business or building experience at all, but I wasn't going to let that stop me. If you put your mind to it, you can do anything.

So I just got stuck into it and did whatever was necessary. I didn't look for reasons not to do something, I just started and sorted out any problems that came up.

Zara looked after our children, and as well she managed the Williamstown Driving School business that came with the house we'd bought in Williamstown. This was a huge help to me because it allowed me to concentrate on AAE matters without having to worry about other things.

Young David standing beside one of the cars belonging to the Williamstown Driving School. Lots of people got their driving licence through this driving school.

...and excited

The factory building had been designed so most of it could be prefabricated which meant it could be quickly assembled on site.

It was like magic; a couple of trucks came and offloaded the steel beams and supports and in not time at all, or so it seemed to me, the builders had erected the framework and put the roof on, and the reinforcing steel mesh was laid down over the floor area.

Once the builders had put up the framework and the roof, it was time for the concrete floor to be poured.

I got so excited I could hardly contain myself when I saw the first concrete truck arrive to start pouring the concrete floor. The overall floor was to be 10 inches deep, which is a lot of concrete. The trucks came in one after the other, and the concreters worked like demons to spread it out and make it smooth and glossy. I wanted to help, but they told me to keep out of the way and let them get on with it.

It seemed that I spent more time here at the factory as it was being constructed than I did at home, at least when the weather wasn't good enough to dive. I still had to dive and bring in my quota of abalone. But as work progressed, I spent many hours doing whatever I could to assist. Whenever I couldn't dive I was on site.

This was the first concrete truck to arrive. It was actually the pumping machine for the concrete. A long hose was used to reach the furtherest corner inside since the actual concrete trucks couldn't go inside the building. The crane on the truck was used to extend the hose inside the building.

The concreters preparing the hopper from which the concrete brought in by the trucks would be pumped through the long hose into the building. As the floor was covered they moved the truck further along. Since the walls on this side of the building had not been erected, access to everywhere inside was easy.

Some could be poured without the pump; and the crane. The truck here could pour the concrete as normal, but it couldn't get to the other side because the wall there had already been erected. They had to pump it across with the long hose on the extended arm of the crane. I became heavily involved and spent many hours doing what I could to assist. Whenever conditions were not good for diving, I was here on site.

The concrete had to be four inches deeper with extra reinforcing where the cool rooms and the freezers were to be located, obviously because when they were full of fish frozen or chilled, their weight would be enormous. No one wanted the floor underneath to crack or collapse.

More than half way done, but still a long way to go.

When the concrete floor had been completed and it had set enough to be able to walk on, work started on putting up the walls and fitting out the interior. The prefabricated wall panels were 4 inch thick polyurethane with white colourbond steel on each side. Each one slotted into place and in no time the building was at lock-up stage. The freezer and cool rooms were constructed with the same material as the walls only they were six and eight inches thick instead of four.

One side almost finished...

From the inside... quite impressive. Still a lot of work to be done. The pipes seen sticking up are for the plumbing of the various machines that have yet to be installed. But... we were making good progress.

Work on our Factory went ahead as planned, except for the odd problems with government and Council Regulations. It would still be a couple of years before it was completed and operational. While the construction continued, we still leased after hours the canning facility SPC had in Collingwood.

Unfortunately, early 1986 part of SPC Collingwood burned down and we were then only able to use the factory to receive abalone for processing. We had to truck it over to another factory used by Monbulk, which was also a part of SPC. It was inconvenient to say the least. Not only that, Victor and his wife were made redundant, but Victor found another job within a few days and to this day we still keep in touch.

Collin still opened the factory for us, to collect and weigh the Abs, and wrote the cheques to pay us.

In the meantime, I had to deal with Ray Town the Manager of Monbulk and his second in charge Bruce Galway, who I found easy to get along with.

It was a turbulent time, especially with the beach price, which went higher by the week. All the processors seemed to have big orders and were fighting for every Abalone they could get their hands on.

I had to pay my divers the same beach price as all the others, otherwise some of them would have sold to the highest bidder.

It was great while it lasted, with everyone making big money, but we were warned that it wouldn't last. I think I paid close to 15 Dollars per Kg in Shell, until I received a letter from Ray Town (from Monbulk) with the new prices they could pay. Apparently, their customers had started to reject the higher prices!

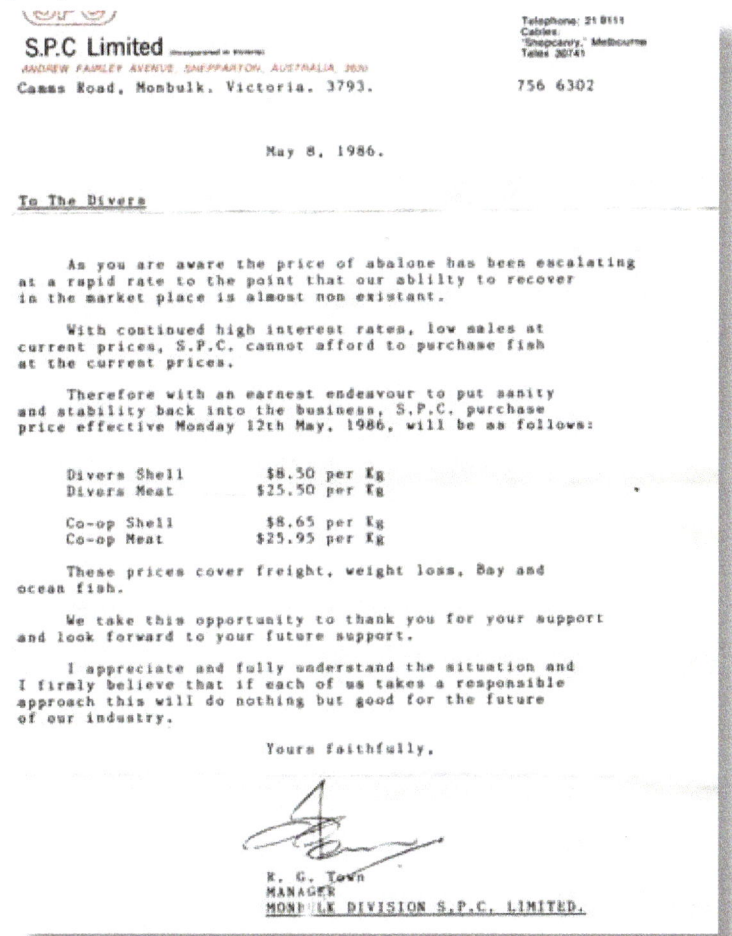

As soon as I had received the letter from Ray Town, the other processors followed suit, and prices everywhere suddenly went down.

It was a huge drop, but we could see it coming and adjusted our finances accordingly. Some of the divers got hit pretty hard and were forced to sell their licence to the highest bidder.

Even though the beach price had dropped considerably, the value of licences kept going up at full speed and after some months, two licences went as high as $300.000.00 each.

That meant $600,000.00 in order to obtain one full licence.

Wow! That was absolutely stunning.

In 1987 Kaz Bartaska, whom I had met many years earlier at SPC, opened his own Export Factory in Kensington, 'Lonimar', with the help of Colin Turner. Kaz had worked with Ardmona and SPC as a sales representative and flew all over the world selling their product, including canned Abalone.

In the beginning, Kaz and his wife Nancy, worked extremely hard to get their product on the market. At first, they found it difficult to get divers to sell to them, being 'newcomers' to the industry, but thankfully, as time went on they overcame these obstacles and succeeded.

At the end of 1987 the last two abalone diving licences were sold for close to half a Million each. By then, there were only 34 Divers in the Central Zone. With that number of divers our reefs could regenerate nicely. At the same time quotas were established at 20.5 ton per licence permitted to be taken, which was a big drop from previous years. The 20.5 ton wasn't too bad, because the beach price kept rising by the week.

In the earlier years, when Ken and I worked together we always finished up with approximately 80 ton between us annually, and when I later worked by myself, I still got between 35 and 40 ton per year. The lesser amount permitted to be taken by each diver guaranteed that the over fished reefs would be able to regenerate, and that, in the long run would benefit every diver as well.

There were big arguments between the existing licensed divers and the 'newcomers' who had bought two existing licences to get into the business.

These new divers went to the Government and argued with them claiming they should be entitled to get double the quota, because they had to pay for two licences, but the existing divers argued that the licence they had was now a single licence, and as such only entitled to a single quota regardless of what they had paid to obtain that licence. In the end the government agreed and everything sorted itself out, and we all found our favourite places to dive and to live!

The Central Zone

It wasn't long before the beach price was 20 Dollars for live abalone, and our annual licence fee crept up to $ 6,000.00 per annum.

Work on the construction of the factory continued and as it neared completion it was time to get stuck into landscaping the surrounds. This was a bit rough at first because the weather had been atrocious and the ground was very wet. We had leased a couple of small machines to help with the landscaping and they often got bogged, horribly bogged, which was awful at the time, but on looking back it now seems rather amusing. Who doesn't enjoy getting covered in mud from time to time?

With help from Billy Nissen and his guys as well as my own family members, my youngest brother in law Paul, and my son David after school, we managed to achieve a lot no matter how messy it sometimes was, and it did get messy, that's for sure.

The Central Zone

Sometimes that damned machine got bogged so deep I thought it would never be released, but the boys always managed to get it free. The bills kept coming in and had to be paid. I still had to pay the divers who sold product to me, and deliver it to cannery we were leasing to be processed. It was a lot of worry, a lot of pressure on me, but I kept pushing through. What had to be done, simply had to be done, and that was it.

When the ground started to dry out a bit we laid the framework for pathways around the factory. More concrete was delivered. I had David and his uncle Paul helping to spread the concrete. The truck stayed well away so it wouldn't get bogged, and used a crane with an extended hose to pour the concrete.

Really starting to look good. Finishing off the first part of the concrete by the main entrance into what would become the fish and chip shop where we would sell fresh and cooked seafood to the public.

    The land had dried out, been leveled and grass planted. A sprinkler system had yet to be installed, but we did create a large graded parking area for visitors as well as workers. Signage was done, and from a distance it all looked good. We still had to bring in the equipment, the pressure cookers, the canning machines, and all the other stuff needed for the processing and production of our sea food products. Getting the equipment in and properly installed was a monumental task, a huge worry, but we achieved it. There was not much I could do here to help. I just had to leave it to the engineers to install everything properly and to make sure it all worked as it was supposed to.
    But it did give me a lot of sleepless nights as I worried about everything.

The Central Zone

A New Era Begins

The pressure cookers had arrived and are being checked by our chief engineer, before taking them inside to be installed.

The pressure cookers installed and ready to start working.

The pressure cookers had their own separate area. They had to be isolated from other working areas because they were pressure vessels, in case of an accident or a sudden release of pressure.

The Central Zone

Above are the abalone washing machines. These were specially designed and built just for us. The pressure cookers were already standard and I made sure the ones we got were fully refurbished and the best that were available.

The four-header Continental food can seamer was made in the USA. I purchased it through my friend Hermann who was the National Service Provider at Containers Limited in Footscray.

This fabulous looking machine is the canning machine. It seals the cans after we've put the contents in.

Most of the ancillary equipment was designed and built by ourselves, whereas, the cookers, steamers and canning machines all had to be bought.

While the equipment was being installed inside the factory, work on landscaping and finishing the outside also went on. We used well established plants so the garden areas gave the impression that they'd been growing for years. I think the guys did a fabulous job, and with the signage on the building looking bright and fresh everything was getting ready for opening and starting operating. It had been an enormous worry for the past few years and it was a relief to see it all coming to fruition.

By the middle of 1987, the resale value of my licence reached one Million Dollars and I was very happy, not only because of that, but also because by then I knew that we would be ready for opening before Xmas. The factory was completed. All we had to do was to run tests to see if everything worked as it was supposed to, and after that we would be ready to start processing our own abalone in our own factory instead of having to lease other canneries to do it. We had already started processing fresh fish for export to Japan so I had finally succeeded in having my own export factory. After working so hard over the last 6 years I couldn't have been happier or prouder of what we had achieved.

Opening Day, 12th December 1987.

I was so excited I nearly wet my pants.

To say opening day was a success would be an understatement; it was fantastic. There were well over two hundred people there which included some of the great people who had helped me along all those past years: people like David Tonkin (Victorian Canneries), Les Tuckey (Melbourne Seafoods), Chris Nadsen (Dover Fisheries and Safcol), Harry Humphrey and Ray Orloff (Smorgons), Colin Turner (SPC), Ray Town and Bruce Galway (Monbulk), and my great friend Bob Bush plus my Greek friend Victor Apostopolus and his family who worked their hearts out to help us. There was also my wife Zara's parents, brothers and sisters and other relatives and friends, too many people to name individually. I hired a small Dixieland Jazz group to entertain the guests which was a great success. My youngest brother in law Paul videotaped the event for posterity.

The amount of food that had been prepared by our five star chef Eric Hemman and his wife Hiang was astonishing. The giant sea food platter in the shape of a fish dominated a whole trestle table and was an absolute work of art.

Photos next page: Guests arriving as the jazz band plays.
Talking with Dr John Silver and Ilse, with my brother in law John
Paul Videotaping, Some of the salads available, Eric and his sea-food platter......>

The Central Zone

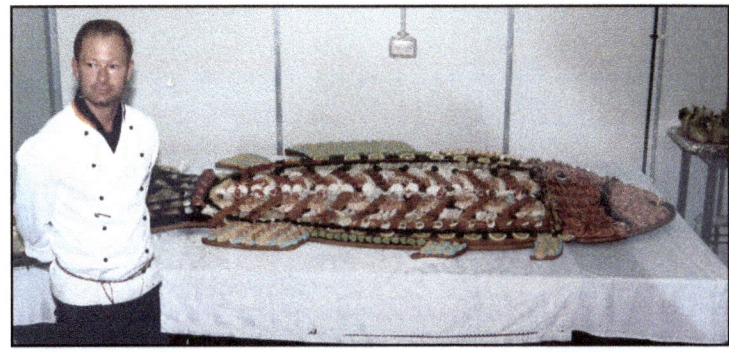

The fish was entirely composed of shrimps and prawns and crayfish and other shell fish, all freshly cooked the night before and arranged as an enormous Platter. Truly a work of art.

Dr. John Silver standing of a wire crate so everyone could see him as he welcomed everyone to the opening.

The amount of food prepared by our chef Eric and his wife was truly astonishing.
I reckon with all that food consumed, no one would be hungry over the coming week.

The Central Zone

Our very good friend, Dr John Silver officially opened the premises with a short speech in which he welcomed the guests and assured them that the food was absolutely first class having been prepared by a five star chef.

We didn't have a ribbon to cut so some wag gave John a smoked eel, and a knife, and he cut this in half while announcing that Australian Abalone Exports was now officially open for business. He wished everybody a great day , and us a great future, and finished by telling everyone they could get stuck into the food.

Which of course they all did, with great enthusiasm.

It wasn't all sea food. Eric also prepared a whole pig roasted on a rotisserie which he is seen here carving portions for the guests lined up.

At the end of the day there was not a scrap of food left, which made me realize just how much people in general loved good sea food. So we started talking about opening our own fish shop as part of the business, but this would be put off for a while, until we established the processing, canning and other stuff we were hoping to do in the factory. Canning took longer than expected. At first, we used the factory for shucking and supplying some of the other processors like SAFCOL, Monbulk and Lonimar.

We eventually set up a special room for guests where our products were on display and where visitors could try a sample. I covered the walls of a dining area with memorabilia from my bike riding days as well as underwater photographs of me diving for abalone so there was something interesting to look at and talk about while they were looking or checking out the products we also sold, this didn't actually happen for another year.

Southern Ocean abalone on a bench waiting to be shucked.

We had to keep everything super clean, all the time. At work in the factory a coupler of days after the opening.

Something different

Immediately after Xmas I was approached by a Korean Guy called Quincy, who wanted to know if we would be willing to supply him with sea urchin roe.

"Can you supply and export them to Korea?"

"Of course we can," I told him, "because we have the divers."

"If you do that I can get some Korean women to come and help prepare the roe."

The Central Zone

It wasn't something I had thought about before, but I knew there were certainly a lot of sea-urchins out there, and they would be easy to collect. We often collected some ourselves when we wanted a quick snack while working out in the Bay.

Funny enough, that was something I first saw my future Brother in Law John and his mate Brian doing when they introduced me to skin diving. I was driving buses at the time and the end of the route was at Williamstown beach near the life saving club. I'd wandered over to take break and to see what was going on, and there were these two guys sitting on the top of the steps leading into the water eating sea urchin roe, fresh out of the water. T

he 'd come out of the Crystal Pool at Williamstown with a bag of sea urchins which they cracked open and were eating the roe when I first saw them and wondered what the hell they were doing. I was intrigued. They gave me a bit to try and although it tasted extremely salty, it was creamy and delicious.

After that, once I'd started diving, I would often get some and crack them open for the roe if I felt a bit hungry.

As soon we got the divers to bring in a load of sea urchins I called Quincy and he sent around the women who quickly sorted, the sea urchins, cut them open and extracted the roe.

Above: good sized healthy sea urchins from Port Phillip Bay. Cut open to display the rich roe.

Right: Sorting the first bins of sea urchins... They were mixed up with abalone taken at the same time.

Friedrich Glasbrenner

A magnificent tray of the finest sea urchin roe from Port Phillip Bay.

With Quincy's help we completed our first export this superb roe and got paid within 3 days.

Quincy was also very interested in frozen Abalone meat. We hadn't yet started any canning of abalone. The system was still being tested, but the freezers were working and we could shuck them and freeze the meat. We were quite happy to sell to Quincy our snap frozen abalone meat.

We worked with Quincy for some time and we had a good relationship, but unfortunately, he had some problems with his people in Korea and had to stop working with us.

I was very sad at the time, but soon got over it when the beach price for our shucked meat had risen considerably and we did very well with that.

In the meantime, we were already processing fresh fish which my good friend Horst Fischer (*his company is Fisher Wholesale PTY*) supplied. It was the freshest Tasmanian Trevally (Snotty Nose) which he caught at night. He got us into selling it at the Tokyo Fish Market. He would bring it in to us very early in the morning and we would pack it into Styrofoam boxes with about 8 fish in each box weighing proximately 20 kilos per box. We used **Qantas** Airfreight containers and each container held 40 boxes. We delivered the containers to the airport and **Qantas** flew them to Tokyo where the fish was sold the next morning at the fish market.

When Horst went fishing, weather permitting, he always saved the last catch for us from which he selected the best fish. This was the freshest fish he caught and this was what we sent to Tokyo. The rest of the fish he caught he would sell to the Melbourne and Sydney fish markets.

The Central Zone

Bruce holding a couple of prime Tasmanian Trevally.

The fish packed into the Styrofoam boxes being inspected by an officer from the Department of Primary Industry before it is shipped to Japan.

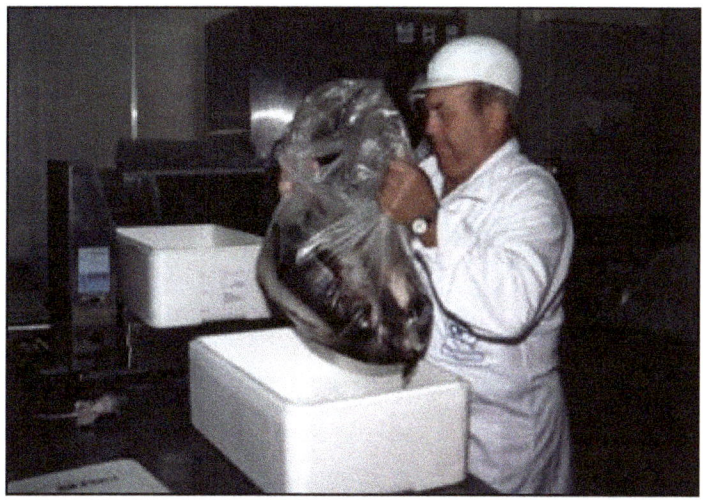

It was a great time and it made me and my "A Team" very happy and especially, when one of the Fish buyers in Japan we were dealing with, told us that our Fish was fresher than the Japanese fishermen could deliver their produce.

Horst also caught by hand some magnificent Tuna from time to time. Whenever he did this he would bring it in to us. We would get it ready for export, also by **Qantas**, to Japan. It would be packed into special cardboard boxes, sealed with a plastic liner and filled with ice. Because the whole fish was quite large, the boxes had to be large as well.

A beautiful Tuna being prepared for packing and sending to Tokyo Fish Market. We called the boxes the tuna was packed in 'Fish Coffins".

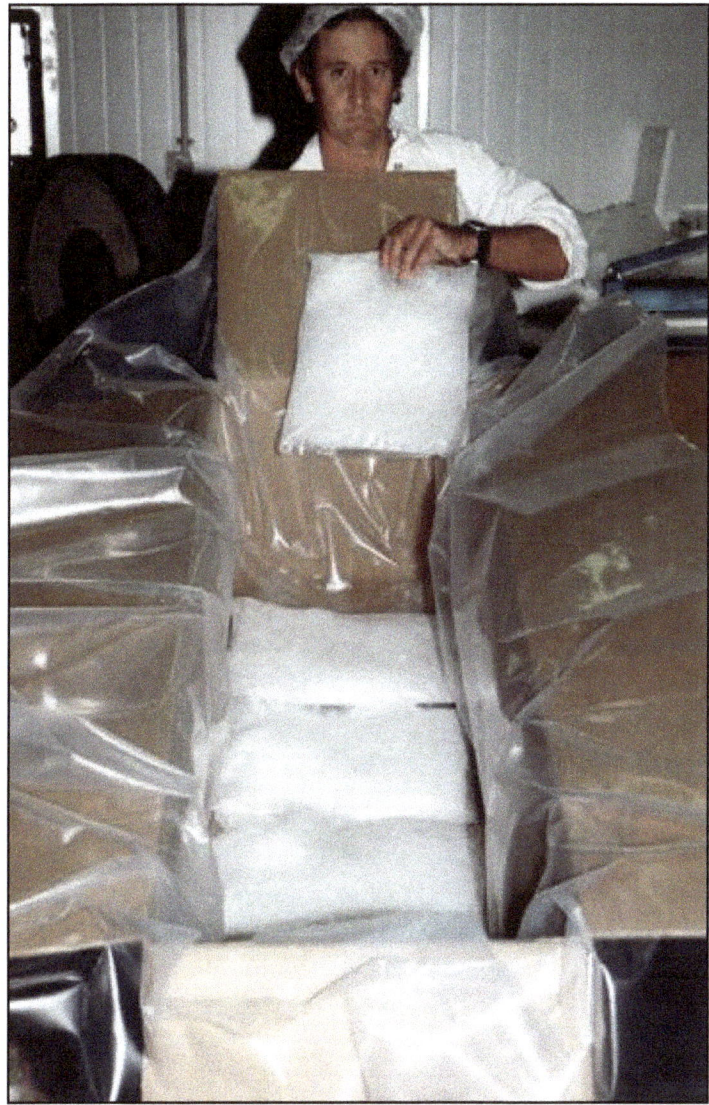

Getting a 'Coffin' ready for another Tuna, packing it with ice.

On average, a fish like the one in the photos would bring us around $4000 each. It showed how much the Japanese valued a Tuna fish. Specimens like the ones caught by Horst were always caught by hand and handled with extreme care so there was no bruising or damage done to the flesh, which resulted in the big prices being paid.

A fish and chip shop

Who would have thought I'd be opening a fish and chip shop?

It was not something that had ever entered my mind. But one day someone suggested the idea. I can't remember who now, but at the time it seemed the logical thing to do.

Up to the moment when we'd decided to try that, we'd only been shucking the abalone we bought from our regular divers and on-selling it to a number of canneries for them to can the product, *and sell it at a further profit for them, not us.* We had been doing this for about a year.

We also had some success with the sea urchin roe, but that stopped because of difficulties Quincy had in South Korea. So when the suggestion arose that we should open a fish shop, it just seemed to be the next natural step.

We were able to get as much fresh fish as we needed. We were already packing and selling fresh fish directly to Tokyo, so why not sell some locally as well?

We created a delightful outdoor eating area which was protected by a covered awning and drop down clear plastic blinds for when Melbourne's notorious moments of sudden bad weather appeared.

We obtained cookers and deep fryers, extra fridges for displaying in the shop a variety of fresh produce. But the main thing turned out to be the cooked fish, chips and other seafoods like scallops and prawns. In no time at all word got around to the local factories, and there were lots of them all around us in the industrial estate, that we had the freshest and the best fish you could buy.

The shop became extraordinarily busy, especially around lunch time as nearby factory workers came here to buy fish and chips for lunch which they would eat in the area immediately outside the shop. We sold heaps of fresh fish too, as well as fresh abalone, so the shop was a good steady income earner.

Never in my wildest imagination would I have thought a shop like that would do so well.

We even had people coming from the other side of Melbourne just to buy our fish because they believed, as did we, that we had the freshest and best fish available, straight out of the ocean the night before.

It was something I was very proud of.

The Central Zone

Our fresh produce on display.
People lined up, waiting for their lunches to be cooked.
Dione and three others hard at work, cooking the fish to be served.

Going great with customers enjoying lunch, or lined up waiting to get into the shop to buy lunch.

Beyond the shop and the outdoor eating area was another entrance into my office and a couple of rooms used for displaying our goods and products as well as a special guest's dining room where we could take our international customers on special occasions. The lunch room was decorated with heaps of photos and memorabilia, all of which were good conversation starters, and the other room was a display room for all of our products.

*David and Shane holding 'fresh flake' (shark) to be prepared for sale in the shop both fresh as well as cooked.
Below: The special guest's lunch room.*

Doing what we were meant to do

Towards the end of 1990 Ray Town informed me that SPC was closing down their Abalone program and from the start of 1991, Monbulk would only concentrate making different Jams.

This was a blow.

I had a meeting with Ray, Bruce, Collin and Bony Jacobs their Chemist, and they offered to help us to start canning in our factory. This was something we'd planned from the start, but we'd got a bit sidetracked after opening the fish shop.

At this point we were approached by the owner of Rainbow Pty Ltd in Taipei City and Kaohsiung City, who was interested in our fresh fish supply and about our canned Abalone.

He told us that as soon as we started, he would pick up a couple of samples to take to Taipei.

Rainbow P/L was the first of our customers, ordering the first pallet of Ocean Gold, by April or May 1991. Actually, everything went pretty smooth and with Bony Jacobs expertise, we had a great product.

My son David managed the production line, overseeing each stage from shucking and sorting the abalone, washing them, putting them into cans, which were then placed in the pressure cookers for cooking. Everything fortunately ran smoothly and we managed a steady production.

David's team, the A team, in action sorting and shucking abalone.

The Central Zone

David and Dione, first in early in the morning getting ready for sorting the day's catch as the divers bring it in. below: The production line in action, Fred checking the cans before they are sealed.

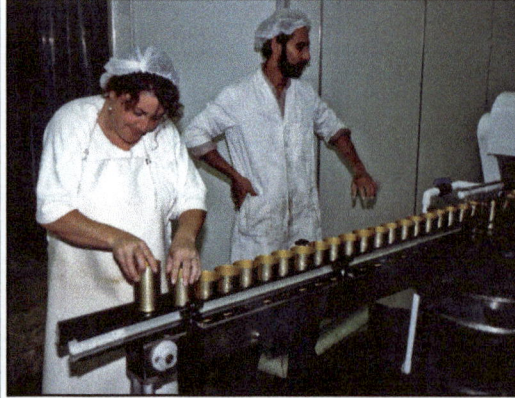

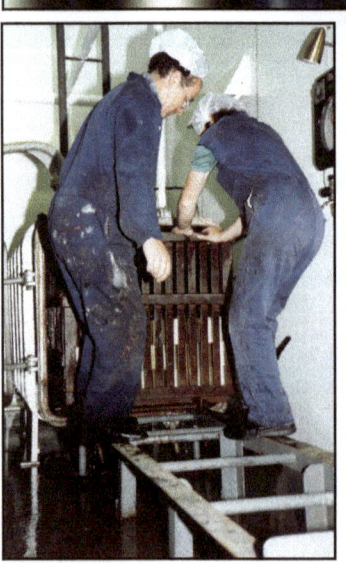

Putting the iron basket of cans into the pressure cooker was not always easy..

Releasing the pressure to enable the cooker to be opened. Taking out the iron bin filled with cooked cans of abalone.

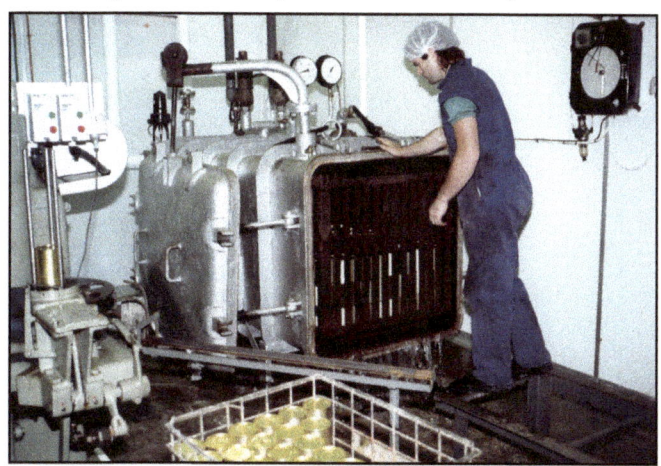

Checking to see all the cans were okay after coming out of the cooker.

Washed and blanched abalone ready to be put into cans.

My very good friend Phillip Tsoi from Chinatown in Melbourne watching the process of canning abalone. He was also a very good customer, stocking many of our products in his shop.

The Central Zone

In this display room we had underwater photos of me abalone diving as well as photos of some products like dried abalone. There was also a collection of old bottles I'd found underwater on different dives. Some of those bottles were more than a hundred years old, so they'd been under the sea for a long time.

Customers from Penang watching our video presentation before buying a selection of our seafood sensations.

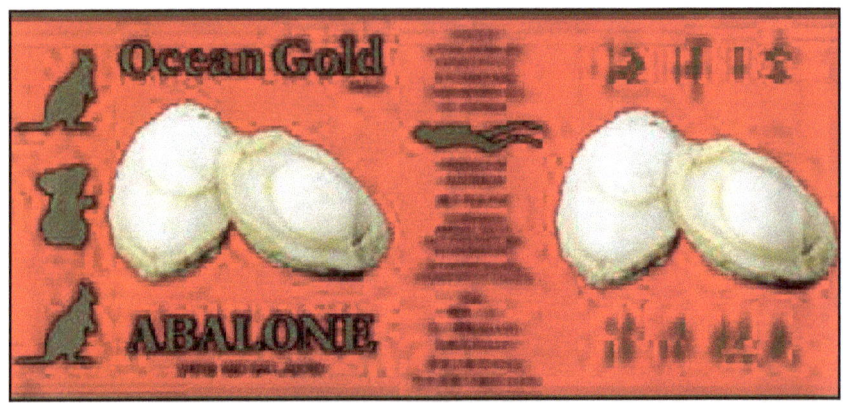

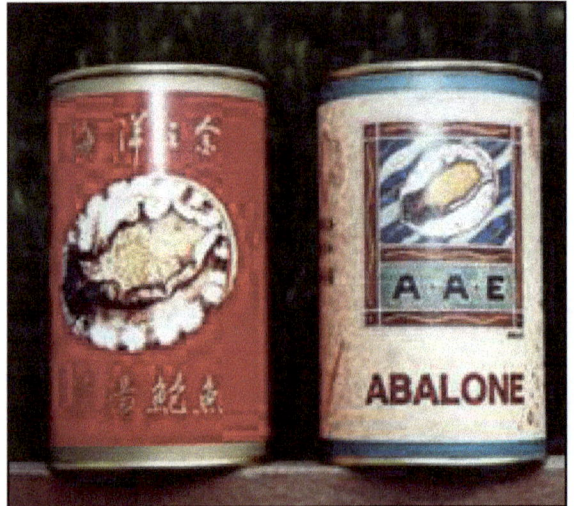

Above: Our first export label.

Middle: Ocean gold for export. Ocean Gold for local sales. Abalone King canned Greenlip.

Left: different labels for different countries and markets.

Below: abalone straight out of a can, on a plate ready to eat.

The Central Zone

Another label again, for export to Germany.

Above: Customers from Taipei watching our promotional video.
With one of my Taipei customers and Ed Lewellen, a DPI Inspector.

Towards the end of 91 Horst Fischer and I decided to travel to Hong Kong and Singapore, Horst to catch up with some Fish suppliers to whom we exported his big Kongo Eels, and myself to find Customers for our Ocean Gold, which eventually we did.

Arriving in Singapore we went straight to Safcol's office to see if they would be interested in our Ocean Gold, but they told us they had to look after their own Brand.

Safcol's Manager sent us to an Industrial area to meet up with the director of Euraco Fine Foods P/L, Sebastian Tan.

Sebastian, was a young hard-working Chinese/Singaporean, who started Euraco in 1987, with his Scottish Abattoir Owner near Aberdeen, John Bain. Euraco concentrated mainly with John Bain's product and imported lots of different European foods.

By the time we met up with Sebastian, he told us he never gave it a thought, adding canned Abalone to his product list, but was willing to give it a go. After opening a couple of our cans, he and his wife Jill were very impressed and Sebastian told me if AAE would only sell to him, he would buy a couple of pallets as soon as we get back to Australia.

What can I say, it only took a handshake and a couple of luncheons to seal the deal and what a great Partnership it turned out to be, for many years.

Horst, Sebastian and Fred today, still the greatest of friends.

The Central Zone

Our export orders were improving all the time and kept the factory very busy with Rainport P/L in Taipei, and Euraco P/L in Singapore being our biggest customers.

We were supported by several divers which enabled us also to supply the odd load to Safcol and Lonimar from time to time.

Two loads, packed and ready for export.

 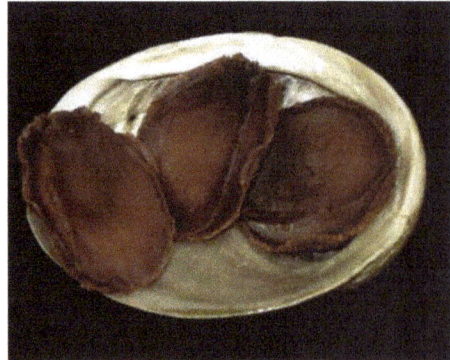

Using a greenlip shell to display some dried abalone.

After lots of patience and many weeks of work and experimentation, we came up with a way of drying abalone and vacuum sealing it in pouches, which turned out to be a success. We sold lots to visiting tourists as well as local customers. We even had it on sale in gift shops at Tullamarine airport.

It was a product I was most proud of.

No longer alone

By then we were no longer alone.

Several other processing factories had opened, like the Abalone Fishermen's Co-operative LTD in Mallacoota. It started operating in 1976 to service the Eastern Zone. Dave Selway started on Phillip Island developing his Abalone retort pouches. The Western Zone Abalone Divers Association started Sou West Seafoods in Port Fairy, and Tassy Warn in Queenscliff along with us in Laverton North.

This expansion of processing factories made it more difficult not only because they were all competing for the same markets, but also because the reefs where good abalone could be found were being depleted. Over-fished, and not given enough time to recover, getting a good supply became ever more difficult. It was worse in other parts of the world. The abalone reefs in California and Mexico had been completely fished out and were basically extinct.

With the beach price in Australia increasing customers who bought abalone from not only us but also the other competitors started looking for cheaper alternatives. They turned to products like the Chilean *Elephant Foot*, (nowhere near as good) and the New Zealand *Paua*, a black fleshed species that had to be bleached before anyone would consider buying it.

While the beach price continued increasing, our license fee remained steady for quite some time, and we were able to concentrate on different products, like canning European Carp, which were plentiful in our Victorian rivers. Horst Fischer caught the Carp with his electro fishing equipment.

Scooping up the stunned carp with nets. With his electro equipment, a current was passed through the water which stunned the fish making them float to the surface where they were simply scooped up. No damage was done to the fish and it was a much better system than netting.

Carp is the most eaten fish in the World, so we knew we had a good market. In one way, we were very fortunate in Victoria, because our Carp had to swim and hunt for their food, not like the farmed carp which were held in ponds and were fed with all kinds of leftovers. Those Carp became very fat, but the Victorian ones were slim, and the fillets were great for canning

We also experimented with smoked fish fillets and retorted Abalone pouches.

Our retorted Abalone pouches did very well on the export marked and we sold heaps through our shop, and in Melbourne's Chinatown to the tourists. At that time, Chinatown was extremely busy with tourists mainly from Asia. Phillip Tsoi, who soon became a good friend took a chance on us and stocked his shop in Chinatown with our premium range of products.

Phillip Tsoi's shop in Little Bourke Street, Melbourne's Chinatown.

Phillip Tsoi speaking with customers in his shop. Behind him our products are prominently displayed, along with photos of abalone diving, the same photos we had on display at the factory.

Shelves in Phillip's shop willed with our premium canned abalone.

A worldwide shortage

By 1993/94 there were Worldwide short supplies of Abalone, canned, frozen or dried. That resulted in huge competitions for the raw product, making it very hard to get. Naturally it was great for the divers, because they could sell to the processors who paid the most.

It was a great time for us, because we could compete with the big companies who would put up the price to the divers before every run of good diving weather. We were lucky that our customers in Singapore, Taiwan and Hong Kong, never complained about the higher price they had to pay, because they wanted to get a lot of our premium product.

I am not quite sure, but by the middle of 1995 we already paid the divers close to $40 Dollars a Kg in the shell and I could sell my licence for 2 million Dollars and by 1998 our yearly licence fee was $54,796.88.

It didn't matter, because we could afford it at the time. AAE was kept very busy.

With the price we paid by 1999 our licence actually dropped to $51,650.38 in 2000.

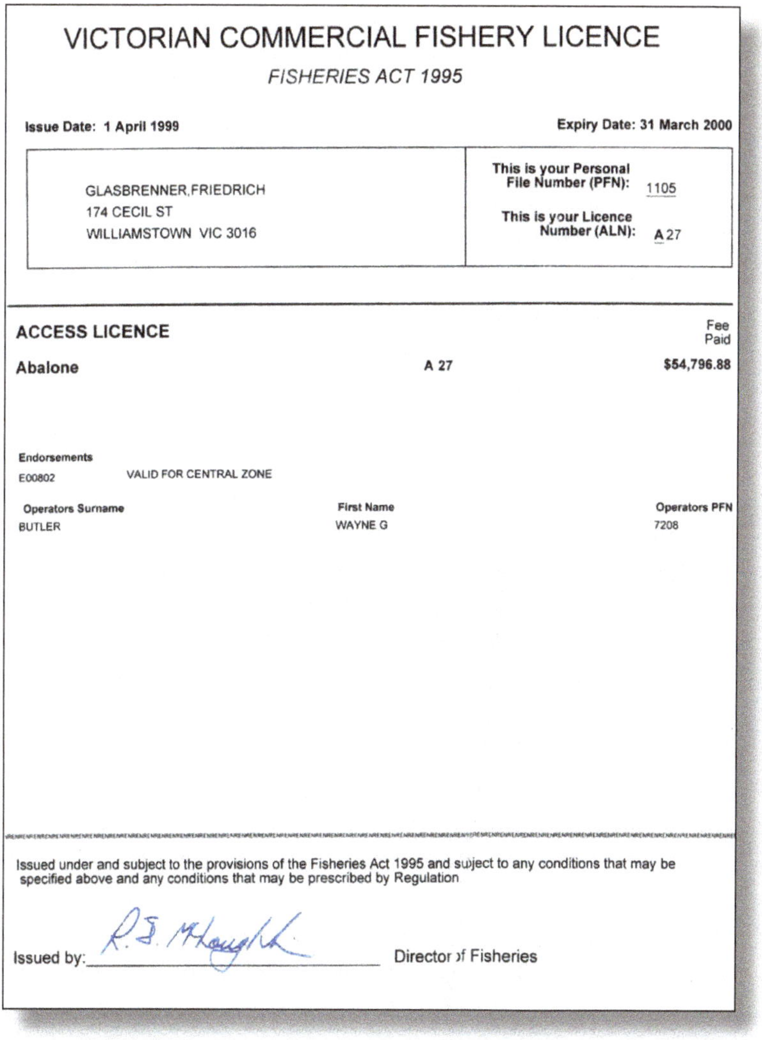

VICTORIAN COMMERCIAL FISHERY LICENCE
FISHERIES ACT 1995

Issue Date: 1 April 1999   Expiry Date: 31 March 2000

GLASBRENNER, FRIEDRICH
174 CECIL ST
WILLIAMSTOWN VIC 3016

This is your Personal File Number (PFN): 1105
This is your Licence Number (ALN): A 27

ACCESS LICENCE   Fee Paid

Abalone   A 27 $54,796.88

Endorsements
E00802   VALID FOR CENTRAL ZONE

Operators Surname: BUTLER
First Name: WAYNE G
Operators PFN: 7208

Issued under and subject to the provisions of the Fisheries Act 1995 and subject to any conditions that may be specified above and any conditions that may be prescribed by Regulation

Issued by: _____ Director of Fisheries

A huge jump from the original fee of $4 back in the 60's which jumped to $200 in 1968, after which it continued to rise steadily until it became what you see above...$54,796.88.

Building the world's largest Abalone.

By the middle of 1997, I came across a Guinness book of records and had the idea of building the biggest Abalone in the World. It had some big things listed in it.

Mentioning it to my family, friends and my staff, they all laughed, but reckoned that it would be a great idea to have a big icon like this in the west.

Once we had it approved by the local Council, which took a long time, we started to get the necessary materials to get on with the project.

At first we had to get some huge Styrofoam blocks and shape them like an Abalone, which took a long time and made a big mess. Once the shape had been done to everyone's satisfaction, Jimmy, our engineer, coated in with fibreglass and then we spray painted it to look like an abalone.

Jimmy also constructed the tower and the rotating mechanism for it.

After more time than you can imagine, the basic shape of the largest abalone was finished. It was then covered with fibreglass and spray painted so it looked like an abalone.

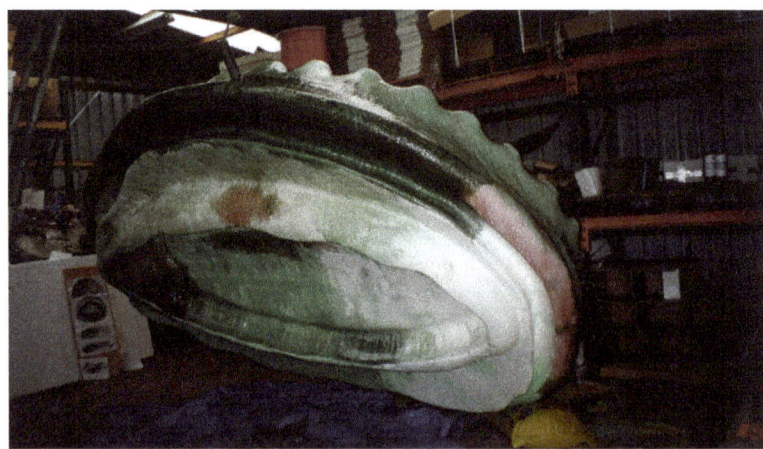

The Central Zone

Above: Finished and ready to be mounted on its tower.
Some of the factory staff with David standing in front of it to give us an idea of its size.

All finished and looking fabulous. I just loved it!

The Central Zone

It must have taken close to one year before we had it on its tower near the front entrance to the block, rotating and looking towards Melbourne.

Finally on the 27th of April 2001, the Honorable Steve Bracks, Premier of Victoria Inaugurated the **World's biggest ABALONE**.

A special plaque was established beside the front entrance to mark the occasion. He declared in his speech that Melbourne was the Abalone Capital of the World.

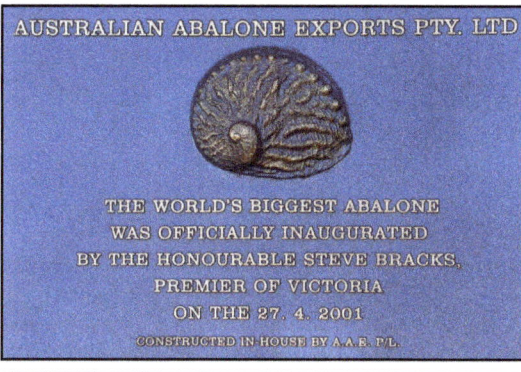

Premier Bracks, Fred, Dione and Jenny waiting to serve the Premier some delicious abalone salad. Below: a plate of my abalone salad, ready to eat.

I approached the Guinness Book of Records about having it included but they refused on the grounds that it was model of something and not the real thing.

"Well of course it's a model. No real abalone will ever grow that big."

David Clarke, the author of Australian Big Things got in touch and wanted to include it in his forthcoming book. He told me it was only one of two rotating Big Things in Australia. The only other one is the World's Biggest Rolling Pin which rotates outside in front of a bakery in Wodonga.

The Central Zone

David Clarke, author of "Australian Big Things" examining the plaque at the front entrance.

Big Abalone

Melbourne, Vic.

Victorian Premier Steve Bracks declared Victoria the 'Abalone Capital of the World' when he unveiled the Big Abalone on 27 April 2001.

Lit up at night and visible from Melbourne's Western Ring Road, the giant 4 metre by 3 metre fibreglass Big Abalone sits on top of a 5.3 metre high tower at Australian Abalone Exports in Laverton North. Designed and built by James Proebstl, it's one of only two rotating Big Things in Australia, along with the World's Largest Rolling Pin at Henri's Bakery in Wodonga.

Australian Abalone Exports Managing Director Fred Glasbrenner wants the abalone to be recognised as the world's biggest. 'We tried to get it into the *Guinness Book of Records* but they wouldn't accept it,' says Fred. 'They said it's only a model. "Of course it is, you stupid bastards," I replied. "So is the Big Banana!"'

Fred is a keen diver and started Australian Abalone Exports with his son David in 1981. In a land of opportunity, he's a huge fan of Big Things.

'Big Things are all about people with passion and vision,' he says. 'People need passion and vision, and if you have that, you pull people along.'

The Big Abalone is located at Australian Abalone Exports, 18–20 Plummer Road, Laverton North. Tel: (03) 9314 4238. Web site: www.aust-ab-exports.com.au

Big Abalone creator, Fred Glasbrenner

The page in David's book featuring our Big Abalone.

No back-pedalling

NEIL KEARNEY on Saturday

For adventurer and risk-taker Fred Glasbrenner, the world is his abalone. And carp. And cycling.

"CARP? They're the best fish in the world, mate." Fred Glasbrenner isn't frightened to back an unfashionable cause.

When Christopher Skase was dying, Fred flew to Majorca to shake the fugitive's hand, because he had just been to a Mirage resort and liked Skase's work.

When abalone licences were $2, and blokes tossed them back arguing two bucks was more than they were worth, Fred kept working his.

A licence that cost $2 in 1966 is worth millions today.

While Aussies poke fun at the kitsch objects we know as Big Things, Fred proudly flaunts the world's biggest abalone, a rotating 5m by 3m erection on a 5m steel tower out front of his Australian Abalone Exports in Laverton North.

"We tried to get it into the Guinness Book of Records, but they wouldn't accept it," Fred says. "They said it's only a model."

"I replied, 'Of course it is, you stupid bastards. So is the Big Banana'."

Now Fred's flogging another unpopular cause — European carp — not to chop up and fertilise the garden, but to eat.

Canned carp. Carp jerky. He's selling carp and exporting it back to his native Germany.

"The healthiest fish in the world — full of omega 3," he says of the illegal immigrant that Australia's waterways.

Whether or not Fred one day erects a monstrous carp alongside his Big Abalone, no one can accuse him of just picking favourites.

Ever since he first ran away from home to join the Foreign Legion, he has taken risks.

The Foreign Legion wouldn't take him — he was too young — but 15-year-old Fred and his 15-year-old friend Theo Guth rode their bikes from their homes near Stuttgart through the Alps into Italy, then sold the bikes to pay for a dinghy to row around the coast of Sicily.

They had no money and teamed up with an Austrian diver whose only possessions were a snorkel, flippers, mask and spear gun.

Fred lived on sea urchins, and to this day rates them the tastiest food he knows.

"Just cut through the middle, take out the gonads with your finger — they're delicious," he says. "Thinking about them makes my mouth water."

FRED was 19 when he decided to come to Melbourne.

He and his friend Theo set out with another boy, Uli Bauer, on bicycles in early December 1955.

They didn't want to alarm their parents, so — instead of declaring their intention to pedal 22,000km through 17 countries to the Melbourne Olympics — they told them they were riding their old bikes to Greece.

Their possessions consisted of a few clothes, sleeping bags, some cooking utensils, and the equivalent of 60 Australian dollars each.

Fred has a picture on the wall of his office that tells the story of their ride.

It's a photo taken on the day they left — three young men in German jumpers — and, with what little cash they had, they made 200 copies of that photograph and turned them into postcards.

They sold the postcards to people they met in return for food and shelter.

Fred laughs that they were too young and naive to consider the venture might not work.

In Syria, a businessman bought one card for five pounds, which would equate to $500 today.

Whenever they passed through a new country, they approached a national or community leader to see their postcards, and to show them the travel journal they were carrying.

They were international visitors, carrying a journal that told the story of their adventure, and it became their passport.

In his backpack, along with clothes and pots and pans, Fred carried the journal and a camera.

By the time they reached Australia, the journal contained photos of them with King Faisal of Iraq, the wife of Indonesian President Sukarno, the trio with the first president of Pakistan, and with the Shah of Persia.

When they left Stuttgart, the only language they knew was a local dialect.

Along the way, they vowed to learn three or four words of English every day.

"We had no idea where Melbourne was," Fred recalls.

"We only knew about kangaroos and koalas."

During their journey, they were hunted by wolves in Turkey, shot pheasants with Arabs, and in Persia were invited to a formal dinner where they were treated to all the local customs.

The polite celebration turned sour when their hosts insisted they drink the local brew, a putrid concoction of rancid milk.

As Fred tells it, the pressure was stifling. Unwilling to drink the stuff — but afraid to offend their volatile hosts — Theo eventually put the cup to his quivering lips and bravely gulped down enough to satisfy the watchful natives.

As he took the cup away to draw breath, a vulture swooped from above and left a dropping in Theo's cup.

Immediately, one of the hosts offered heartfelt apologies to Theo, filled his cup again, and insisted that — seeing he had enjoyed the first drink so much — he must swallow some more.

WHEN the trio reached Indonesia, they somehow talked their way into tea with Ibu Fat Mawati, wife of President Sukarno.

She even convinced the Indonesian government to pay their air fares from Jakarta to Darwin.

Of all the remote and able places they visited, daunting was Darwin.

Within an hour of landing in the Northern Territory, to catch a plane back to...

Fred remembers wilder than any town ined from the cowboy...

"We rode our bicycle ing on a corner, and we were horses tied up to...

A radio played horses in shorts and singlets w bets, and the bar threw the three Ge when they asked in h English if they could drinks. "What?" the yelled. The pub went m

"If you want Coca barman scalded "Fin milk bar."

They got on their rode south, and months — found a come in Melbourne.

"It was another world for me — the wonderful unknown of the sea. To this day, I still can't wait to put my head under and dive into the unknown." — Fred Glasbrenner on his introduction to diving

---

There was always a reporter willing to write a story about me, or about abalone diving or anything local that could help fill a newspaper, and I was always happy to oblige. Neal Kearny came out to AAE to interview me for a feature article over lunch and he got the whole story.

Neal took me literally and wrote down everything I told him, even what abalone does for the health of elderly people.

The Central Zone

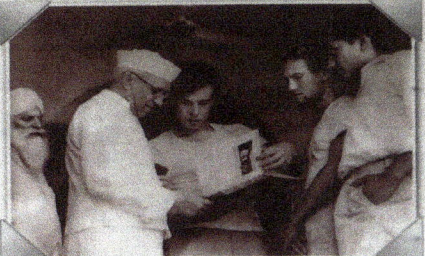

or free spirit Fred

Fred, Theo and Uli with their bikes, in Indonesia, Germany...

...diving opened up a new world for the enterprising Fred ...nner, who now turns over $3 million a year at his abalone ...g business.

...red proclaims Melbourne as the abalone capital of the world.

ANDREW TAUBER

...all stayed on after the Games. Uli got married ...bourne girl, but left after ...ars, and lives in Vienna ...went back to Europe via ...ndu, where he became with the King of Nepal and ...ated Hilary.
...sees Uli and Theo at least ...ery year in Europe, and a ...as launched in their German town last month to their overland adventure 50 years ago.
...liked Melbourne so much after the Olympics — he got ...riving buses from Moonee ...o Williamstown.
"Y day he watched a ...ar-old schoolgirl get on at Yarraville and get off at ...ay station. She was a ... and later became one of ...ous Lido girls."
...he grew to know her, he ...ake the girl, Zara Litchen, ...ree ride on his bus at ...ch, and he was still driving ...when he married her in 1964.
...a brother, John, took them ...n the bay or at Barwon ...and Fred enjoyed the ...ater world so much he ...uses in the morning and ...ed for six or seven hours in ...rnoon.
...as another world for me — ...nderful unknown of the ... says. "To this day, I still ...at to put my head under ... into the unknown."
...65, he started diving for ... "Aussies called it mutton ... they reckoned it wasn't ...od for bait."
...yone frowned on us ab...vers — we slept in tents on ...ch and lived like bums."
...e mid-1960s, divers raided ...beds. Fred says they were ...um cleaners.
...lean up the industry, the ...overnment in 1968 raised ...nce fee from $2 to $200, and ...of the thousands of divers ...the licences were worth

the new fee. The rest went back to their old jobs.
Fred thought hard about going back to full-time bus driving, but Zara had a job to support him, so he and a mate, Ken Johnson, borrowed $400 from a bank to buy their licence.
"People say we were lucky," he says. "But this is a land of opportunity — we took our chance."
Fred has spent 18,000 hours underwater diving for abalone.
He established Australian Abalone Exports in 1981, built a factory with son David, and turns over $3 million a year, mostly exporting to Asia.
He says abalone is so important to Asians because it is a tradition.
"If somebody gets married they must have abalone, shark fin, sea cucumber or fish stomach on the table or they lose face."
The best way to cook abalone, he says, is quickly.
"If you haven't got an erection in 10 minutes (after eating it) there's something wrong with you."
He is proud of his Big Abalone, built by engineer mate Jimmy Proeboti, which bears the proclamation: "Welcome to the Abalone Capital of the world, MELBOURNE."
The Big Abalone stars in a new book, Big Things, by David Clark, standing alongside Australia's other larger-than-life attractions.
Almost 50 years after his epic ride from Germany, Fred still loves cycling.
He took over from E.J. Whitten as patron of the Footscray Cycling Club, and on his factory wall he has a framed yellow jersey that Lance Armstrong wore in his first Tour de France win.
It hangs near that prized picture of the three young men in the German jumpers, the portrait that became a postcard that paid Fred's way to his life in Australia.
kearneym@heraldsun.com.au

I was very proud of my son David for his help and enthusiasm over the years we worked hard to establish AAE.

Friedrich Glasbrenner

The Man-made Artificial Reef of Altona

We designed most probably the first successful underwater artificial reef for abalone.

At that time Professor Peter Hanna, who taught at Deacon University in Geelong, rang and asked me to visit him at the University. He told me he wanted to show me some small Abalone which he and his team had hatched in medium sized tanks in a shed next to the bay in Geelong.

I was really surprised when I saw hundreds of small Abalone as little as a fingernail sticking on roof tiles and bricks, being fed with fresh seaweed. Peter told me that he would be able to produce millions of tiny Abalone, by collecting their sperm and then letting it settle under the right conditions.

After several visits and getting to know each other, we concluded that we should build the first man made natural reef for abalone in the World, and we decided the best place with easy access was near Altona in Port Phillip Bay.

A concrete company not far from AAE, designed with our input, a mould where concrete mixed with crushed basalt and scoria could be poured. The reef had to seem natural for the weed to grow and Abalone to settle.

With the help of Kaz Bartaska from Lonimar, who wrote numerous letters to the Government Departments, visited several Ministers and had lots of discussions, we finally received a three year development lease in Altona Bay between the Point Cook Homestead and the old ammunition pier.

We had to sink our blocks away from existing Abalone reefs which had to be checked by the Fisheries.

We selected an area a kilometre or so offshore where the bottom had no growth, only small pebbles and sand. It was also an area less likely to be visited by amateur fishermen. It was ideal because it would be easy to see and document how the artificial reef evolved.

The blocks were enormously heavy and with the boats at our disposal we could only take one block at a time out to the location where we would drop it onto the bottom.

Once underwater the divers could stack blocks on top of each other so create nooks and holes where small abalone could hide from predators like starfish and leather-jackets which would surely discover the reef in their search for food.

The Central Zone

Getting the first block to sit on the rubber dinghy without tipping over was a job in itself. It was wedged in place with several empty plastic containers, and tied down, then pushed out so it floated freely. After that, a tow rope was attached and we used another boat to tow it out to the location.

Making sure the dinghy doesn't bounce too much as it is towed out, by another boat.

The block is over, and they had to go back for the others, one at a time until the reef was finished.

The Central Zone

Three views of the first six blocks laid down for the reef. It took six trips and all day just to get these out there, underwater, and stacked up to form the base for a reef.

We actually transplanted some sea weed from another reef next to our man made reef to encourage it to grow faster.

We monitored it each week and found it took roughly three months for the weed to start growing on our reef.

Below: the first sea weed on the reef. It didn't take long after that for things to start appearing. More seaweed, little fish, dollar stars, so it was time to seed it with some baby abalone.

Wayne Butler holding a roof tile on which Professor Peter Hanna had grown his abalone in tanks near Geelong.
The tiles had been placed in the tank as they would been on a roof and it immediately attracted the small abalone to the underside where it was not exposed to the water above.

Several roof tiles on which Professor Peter Hanna had been growing his farmed abalone were carefully placed on the reef. We wanted to see whether they would migrate off the tiles onto the reef structure, now that it was covered with a layer of fine sea weed. Rock ling and other fish had already discovered the reef and were living in it for protection. It seemed about right to put some abalone there to see how they would go.

The Central Zone

Unfortunately, the predatory starfish, *Coscinasterias Calamaria*, must have smelled them and came from who knows where, and made short work of these few small abalone. We waited a couple of weeks after that and since the starfish had moved on we decided it was time to seed the reef. We placed up to a thousand juvenile abalone on the reef and couldn't believe how quick they grew. It only took 22 months for them to be legal size of 100 millimetres.

We had big plans, like building U shaped pontoons for overseas tourists to dive on and take some live abalone back to their families and proudly being able to tell them that they dived for them in Altona Bay Victoria. We also envisioned that we could have a laboratory and aquarium on the pontoons to teach the public all about the underwater life in Port Phillip Bay. Of course the reef would have to be extended in order to do some of that, but now that we had done it, that wouldn't be a problem.

I was full of ideas for possible future developments.

I had a great time with Peter and his team, who developed a state-of-the-art laboratory in a movable 20 foot container, also financed by Peter and myself, to create millions of juveniles to reseed the existing reefs on our coastline.

I should also mention here that we had holding tanks back at AAE where we kept a number of live abalone for customers who particularly wanted live abalone to cook and not canned or dried abalone. We also supplied shops and some restaurants in Chinatown with live abalone which they kept in aquariums in their shop front for customers to select an individual one either to take home or to have cooked right there in the restaurant.

Wayne Butler used his boat, seen above, to take a couple of politicians out to the reef to see how it was doing once it had been well established. It was black lip abalone that we were going to seed the reef with. The boat's name reflected the abalone that Wayne usually dived for, Black Lip.

Friedrich Glasbrenner

Peter was not only a successful breeder of abalone, he also enjoyed a great drop of wine. Seen here in our guest lunch room at AAE with a bottle of the finest which we opened for my 70th birthday.

Below: Peter and Kenny holding superb blacklip abalone which we were keeping in our holding tanks for customers who wanted fresh live abalone.

 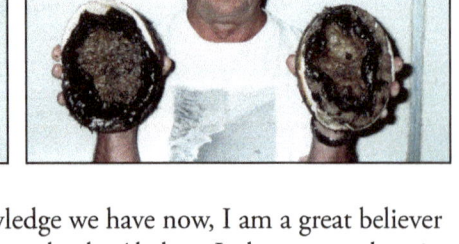

To this day, because of the knowledge we have now, I am a great believer in reseeding depleted reefs. Unfortunately, the Abalone Industry members in Victoria weren't behind us, and I still can't believe that the quota holders are happy with losing so much of their possible future income.

Peter and I had spent a huge amount of money, with the help of Deacon University, to create something unique.

Within three years we had size Abalone all over our blocks, even young ones in every crevice to keep safe, which were born naturally.

We were looking forward for our first harvest, maybe a 100 kg for starters, when I had a visit from the Fisheries Department, during lunchtime at AAE.

Having lunch with several of my staff, we invited him to join us, but he declined. I have forgotten his name, but he turned out to be a typical bureaucrat, flaunting his authority.

He told me that he and the department wouldn't continue to renew our permit.

After questioning him for the reason why, he told us that it was "detrimental for the environment."

We were dumbfounded, especially when he told me, with a smirk on his face, that I should go out and clean up our mess.

Our mess!

Well, that was it! I couldn't believe what came out of his mouth.

It made my blood boil.

"Okay," I told him in a subdued voice, "you people want us to clean up a pristine reef, which we created out of nothing, with great effort and enormous cost. You must be kidding! "

I waited for him s to say something else but he remained silent, blank faced.

"This is a reef where schools of Snapper appeared out of nowhere, where juvenile Leather-jackets swim in my open hands, with sand whiting searching through the reef. To top it off, there are pods of Porpoises visiting us frequently, and sometimes you can put your arm around the odd one."

Everyone in the lunchroom stared at this idiot, unable to comprehend what he wanted us to do.

"I tell you what," I said looking him straight in his eyes, "Why don't you, with your wages go down off Mornington and clean up the so-called reef, which you people built out of old tyres and taxpayers' money, which to this day still pollutes Port Phillip Bay. When you do that, then we shall demolish our pristine Reef!"

To this day I never heard from him again, but he left his legacy.

We were not allowed to continue with our project of seeding artificial reefs with abalone that we could sustainably farm. How could what we were doing be considered detrimental to the environment? That is the question this bureaucrat or any one else in his department could not answer. But they were adamant that we had to stop whatever we were doing.

When I told Peter the bad news, he was so disappointed, that after some months he went to Thailand and worked with the Bangkok University.

He died a few years later years. Maybe of grief; at least that's what I think.

I must mention one more thing in regard to this which shows how some state governments are more open than others to new ideas that could see people developing something new that brings both work, money and tourists, from which everyone involved benefits.

Brad Adams, Ocean Abalone Rancher

Brad was an abalone diver in West Australia for many years, before he decided to come and visited us, with his dad Terry, his mum Flo and brother Nathan, at AAE. Apparently, they had heard about us and our foresight in building an underwater reef to grow and protect abalone.

They spent several days in Melbourne, and we showed them pictures and drawings of our once future prospects and they thought it was fantastic. We had some great lunches together while we talked of future possibilities.

To this day, we still keep in touch. Brad often reminds me about the great lunch they had, and how he'd had difficulties walking in a straight line towards their taxi afterwards. Brad reckons we fed them too much Schnapps.

They went back to WA and put a proposal about **Abalone Ranching** to the WA Government and got permission to start an underwater ranch near Augusta, a small town on the far south-west coast of Western Australia where the Blackwood River enters Flinders Bay. It has a population of around 1000 people.

A first class greenlip abalone, like the two Brad is holding. These are the best abalone and the most favored across all of Asia.

Brad Adams, Ocean Abalone Rancher.
Holding two of the typical green lip abalone he grows on his artificial reef in the Great Southern Ocean near the town of Augusta. WA.

The Central Zone

Greenlip abalone growing and foraging on Brad's reef while a fish swims past.

Brad surfacing with a bountiful harvest of fine greenlip abalone from his artificial reef.

Brad and his team became extremely successful, growing mainly Greenlip Abalone for the local and export market. Brad is now producing the same amount of abalone as the whole of the West Australia quota catch, an astonishing feat!

This is the difference between farsighted West Australia, and short sided Victoria.

To this day I still feel very sad about our missed opportunity.

But life goes on...

Being increasingly busy over the couple of years since we opened the factory, I transferred my licence to my Niece's husband Wayne Butler, who has been working with us for some time. Wayne turned out to be one of the best divers and took a lot of pressure of my back.

Wayne and his deckhand returning on a cold morning after diving in freezing water.
He had a good catch and is seen here filling in the necessary documents for reporting to the Fisheries Department.

The Central Zone

Wayne Butler, finished with the paperwork. Thinking about going home for a hot shower and a stiff drink.

With Wayne taking care of the diving, I was free to concentrate on finishing the surroundings of the factory, because tourist buses started to frequent us with loads of Asian tourists who couldn't get their hands on enough of our abalone products.

Palm trees had to be planted, a 5-star toilet block was built, driveway and car park for customers as well as another for staff, and entrance gates erected. I was particularly proud of our fine entrance with its beautiful wrought iron gates and fences. The transformation from what had once been an empty lot full of grass and weeds was a dream come true.

Our shop with all the fresh seafood available to us, became busier by the day and the team at the factory, opened by David, started at 3 am most of the time. When the weather was good for diving, I usually received the Abs late in the evening.

A surprise package.

At the end of 1999 or early in 2000, I received a big envelope from the Bremen University, containing documents and a long letter from a Dr, Monika Fritz, a Professor at the Bremen University, inquiring about Greenlip Abalone shells.

Apparently, she was being financed through the **Volkswagen Foundation** to develop a paint using Mother of Pearl, for Environmental reasons.

I got in touch with Dr. Monika and told her that it was a great idea, and I would like to help in any way I could.

She asked if it was possible for us to send a few boxes of Greenlip shells to Bremen and the University would gladly pay for them.

"Don't bother. I am happy to help."

We did send the shells, but they had a problem with customs in Germany. After a fax from us explaining the availability and catch rate, they had no more problems.

I rang Monika and told her that in a few weeks' time I was leaving for Germany to go to Stuttgart and told her that my brother would gladly drive me to Bremen to meet up with her at the University, which we did.

What a surprise we got when we arrived and met Monika and her team of several scientists and a handful of students; we were treated like VIPs.

The paint they were developing would be revolutionary because mixing mother of pearl with the finished product would be incredible. This paint could be used for thousands of applications like big ships, tankers, roofs on houses, or cars and many more, because nothing grows on Mother of pearl.

Not being a scientist, I was mesmerized by the dedicated work these people were doing. Apparently Greenlip were easier to work with than Blacklip or other shells, because of the way they are formed and held together. Some other shells were brittle, compared to greenlip.

Young Susanne, an up-and-coming scientist, actually took pictures through an Electron Microscope, emailing me the results.

I found it quite incredible to look at the inside of a greenlip shell.

It never occurred to me, nor my friends and divers to find out anything about the inside of a shell. After half a century of diving, all we were after was the abalone meat.

Friedrich Glasbrenner

Professor Monika Fritz with her two sons.
Above:: Suzanne Jordan Professor Monika's assistant who took the photos below. She is in our back yard holding an Ocean Gold can, and a greenlip shell.

Below are 4 of the remarkable electron microscope photos of the mother of pearl inside an abalone shell. I don't think any divers or processors have ever seen pictures like these. Who would have thought that the shell was made up of countless microscopic layers.

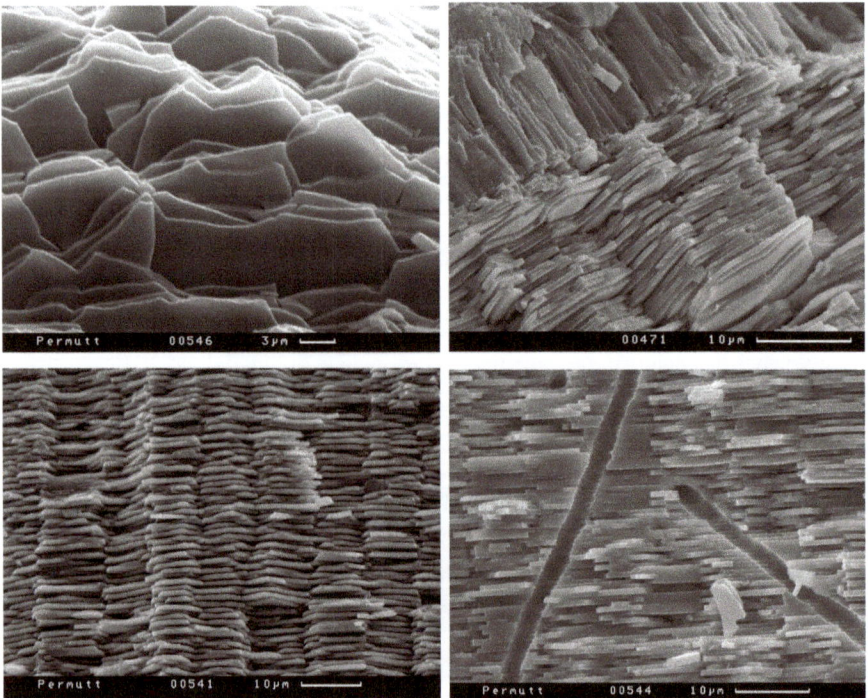

The Central Zone

Suzanne Jordan about to explore Port Phillip Bay at Williamstown and several abalone reefs.

Every time I look at the electron microscope photos Suzanne sent me they send shivers down my spine. Just holding an empty shell and seeing how glossy and smooth it is, and then thinking what is there that the human eye can't see, also sends shivers down my spine. Nature is amazing. The two channels in the fourth photo on the previous page are made by microscopic worms that live within the shell itself.

Suzanne was sent to Australia, to learn about Abalone, and through an invitation from Peter Hanna, she stayed at the Deakin University campus in Geelong for a couple of weeks and learned a lot from Peter and his team.

For or another 5 weeks she stayed with us and we were able to show her some great places in Melbourne and around Victoria.

The following summer in Germany, I visited them again, but this time I took Zara and we stayed nearly two weeks.

Again we were treated like royalty!

New Customers

We had taken part in a couple of Food and Beveridge Expos, the first in 1992 with our Friends Sebastian and Jill from Euraco Pl. and in 1994 with Jeffrey Tan from International Premier Foods Pty Ltd both in Singapore.

At the 1994 Expo one of the Singaporean Importers asked me if I could sell canned and frozen Abalone to him? I told him that we were doing business with Euraco, but they were only selling to the big Hotels in Singapore and Malaysia, but not to Chinese restaurants. I handed him my card and told him if he is interested in dealing with the local Chinese, I would love to supply him.

I never heard from him for a long time, until a couple of years later he turned up with his wife and son at our factory. Well, that was a surprise, because I had totally forgotten about him and couldn't even remember his name.

Peter Chua, his wife and son Kelvin, trying some of our products.

Peter was a small Importer with only one employee, but had lots of connections, having been employed by the Singapore Government previously. Peter became a valuable customer for us and bought a pallet of Ocean Gold just about every week.

Peter, like most of our customers kept complaining every time the price went up, but it was not our fault, because the beach price kept going up and up. As a matter of fact, by 1999 we had to pay a lot of money for our yearly Licence.

The 3rd National Abalone Convention

In 2005 the Tasmanian Abalone Industry organized the 3rd National Abalone Convention in Hobart, where one could catch up with people, from all over Australia and some other countries, who were involved with Abalone.

It was a great success.

Michell Hansen and her Father Alan were there.

Alan, from Tasmanian Seafood's PL was the most recognized entrepreneur in the Abalone Industry Worldwide! Alan was the Number one guest speaker, plus several more. As funny as it may sound, but Alan and I were the same age and both of us were born in America. Many times, we had discussions about our early lives.

Soon Lee and myself having a great time in Hobart.

Fred, with Gwendolin and Frank Mathews. It was great to catch up with them again. Frank was the first person to make cans of abalone soup way back when I was first starting out as an abalone diver.

Selling AAE, the final chapter.

I'll never forget the day when I flew back to Melbourne after that convention in Hobart, when someone sat next to me on the vacant seat and offered me 7 million dollars for my Access license and quota units. He said he would write me out a cheque right away, right there while we were still on the plane back to Melbourne.

I was dumbfounded and couldn't believe what I just heard, because at that time I would have been paid more than any other licence sold before. Unfortunately, I declined his incredible offer.

With our factory working full on and our shop unbelievable busy, I was extremely happy with what we had created, and I was grateful with my perfect Team.

We supplied just about half of our local products to Phillip Tsoi, who owned a retail shop in Little Bourke St (Chinatown). The balance was sold locally in our own shop, or exported to various Asian destinations as already mentioned.

It was an amazing time, and by 2006 we paid 50 Dollars per live Kg to the divers.

At that time the licence fee was just over 57 thousand Dollars per year. It didn't matter, because by that time we received 150 Dollars for 1 Kg of shucked meat, plus we sold each can of our export Ocean Gold for 50 Dollars. In some places it even sold for 70 dollars a can.

I can still remember, when some of the divers told me, that I would soon have to pay them 100 dollars for one Kg to get their Abalone! And all the divers agreed.

By the middle of 2008 we had to pay the divers 57 dollars a live Kg and that's when the bubble burst.

To top it all off, a virus called "*Ganglioneuritis*", started to destroy the Abalone Industry and that frightened the living daylight out of me and many others. It was accidentally introduced into the wild reefs by seeding them with farmed abalone. It spread like wildfire and decimated reefs along the Victorian coast.

The future looked bleak for the abalone diving industry in Victoria.

I put AAE on the market and was approached by Elders to see if I could come to an arrangement with them, because they owned a company *"ISD International Seafood Distributors"* and would be interested in buying our Business.

They made me a reasonable offer for the factory and my Licence, but I kept my Greenlip Quota, which I still have to this day and the rest is History.

Looking back over all those years, I had a fantastic time and met a great number of friends along the way, and it saddens me, that we had lost a lot of our original divers and friends, may they rest in peace.

But I wouldn't change a thing if I had my life over again; well, in retrospect, perhaps just one thing I would change; I should have accepted the 7 million dollar offer given to me on the plane flight back from that convention in Hobart.

But life is what it is, what we make it, and we have to live with it.

That's all there is...

"Hail to The Queen of the Ocean, ABALONE"

Kenny just loved sharing a stubby or two.

Fred (Friedrich Glasbrenner) with his underwater video camera.

Acknowledgments

My Brother-in-law, John Litchen, without his help I wouldn't be able to finish this book.
Cecil Cheng, who started the Abalone Industry.
Ken Johnson, my long-time diving partner and Friend.
The great Bob Bush, first skipper on the Mintak and the great diving friends I made at the time!
Less Tuckey owner of Melbourne Seafood's.
Ray Orloff and Harry Humphreys from Smorgans,
The management of SAFCOL.
Collin Turner, manager of SPC in Collingwood Who helped me along the way, plus Victor and Jenny Apostopolous.
Kaz Bartaska and his wife Nancy, former owners of Ionimar, now Kansom.
Hermann Hitzler, who was able through his company to supply us with the best can closing machine available.
Wayne Butler, one of the best divers, who married my niece, Heike.
Plus, David Tonkin who started with Victorian Canneries and for many years after, became the Secretary of the Abalone Processors Association.
To Sebastian and Jill Tan owners of Euraco Pty Singapore who helped us, become successful.
Alan Buck who supported us from the start to the end and I shall never forget the diving Adventures we had together.
John Thynne, who was with me from the start of AAE. John became a great friend, and I shall never forget when he and Robyn, his Partner, celebrated with me on my 50th birthday in Germany.
Finally, my wife Zara, who put up with me over all those years, for giving me the freedom to succeed.
Many years later my son David, who learned very quickly how to manage AAE and worked his butt off.
And of course, the fabulous A Team; I am still in touch with some of them to this very day.
Thank you all; you have made my life the wonderful experience that it has been.

*Fred, Ken, and John, at Finschhafen in
New Guinea, 1970.*

www.ingramcontent.com/pod-product-compliance
Lightning Source LLC
Chambersburg PA
CBHW041312240426
43669CB00023B/2970